PREVIOUS BOOKS

Spiritual Wisdom for Peace on Earth From Sananda channeled through David J Adams

LOVE IS THE KEY,
PART 1

SPIRITUAL WISDOM FROM GERMAIN

CHANNELED THROUGH DAVID J ADAMS

DAVID J ADAMS

authorHOUSE®

AuthorHouse™
1663 Liberty Drive
Bloomington, IN 47403
www.authorhouse.com
Phone: 1 (800) 839-8640

Published by AuthorHouse 08/17/2018

ISBN: 978-1-5462-5593-2 (sc)
ISBN: 978-1-5462-5591-8 (hc)
ISBN: 978-1-5462-5592-5 (e)

Library of Congress Control Number: 2018909804

Print information available on the last page.

Front cover Photo called "Marine Meditation Light Explosion" was taken by Kath Smith at the Marine Meditation in September of 2012.

Back cover Photo was taken on the camera of David J Adams, the T shirt was created by Tie Dye artist, Ruth Cary Cooper from USA.

<u>DEDICATION</u>

I Dedicate this book to my children, Nicky and Suzi, my grandchildren, Lauren, Matthew and Emily, and my great grandchildren, Ruby–Rae and Peyton, for they and others of the next generations will carry the Light forward and create the Peace that we all yearn for.

ABOUT THE AUTHOR

ADAMS, David John Patrick

Born: 28th April 1943

At: Mountain Ash, Glamorgan, South Wales, UK.

Moved to South Australia in 1971, Currently living in the southern suburbs of the city of Adelaide.

Began his Spiritual Journey as a result of the Harmonic Convergence in late 1987.

In 1991, he was asked by Beloved Master Germain to undertake a global Meditation based on, and working with, the Consciousness of the Oceans, which was called the Marine Meditation.

In 2009 he was asked to address a Peace Conference in Istanbul to speak of the Marine Meditation and his work for World Peace through meditation.

He is a Songwriter, a Musician, an Author and Channel, but most of all a **SERVANT OF PEACE**.

David began bringing through information from a variety of Masters and Cosmic Beings in the form of Meditations around 1991. It was not, however, until after the year 2000 that he began to channel messages in group situations and in individual sessions. Most of these messages were not recorded or transcribed so remain shared with only a few people, but in 2009 the messages being brought through in the weekly Pendragon Meditation group began to be recorded and transcribed by Kath Smith and sent out around the world on David's own Pendragon network.

David's special Guide and Mentor has been 'The Germain, the I am that I am', but he has also worked extensively with – and channeled - Sananda, Hilarion, Djwahl Khul, AA Michael, The Merlin, The Masters of Shambhala, as well as Arcturian Sound Master Tarak and his own Home Trinity Cosmic Brother Ar'Ak.

(Contact email – djpadams8@tpg.com.au)

ACKNOWLEDGEMENTS

I, David J Adams, would like to acknowledge three special Earth Angels.

Heather Niland/Shekina Shar - who helped me to awaken to my Journey in 1987 and connected me to my Beloved Friend "The Germain", she was a mentor, guide and teacher way ahead of her time.

Meredith Pope – who walked in the same shoes as me in those difficult early years as a fellow 'weekender' at The EarthMother Centre, and was - and still is - an inspiration to me.

Krista Sonnen – An Harmonic and Earthwalker, who helped to build the bridges to my Spiritual and Cosmic friends by persistently urging me to allow them to speak through me in private sessions, then in group sessions. Without her support these messages would not be here.

I would further like to acknowledge **Kath Smith** – A spiritual Being of immense Love and Joy who initiated the recording and transcribing of the messages received in Pendragon so that the messages from our 'other Dimensional friends' would not be lost forever. Also **Takara Shelor,** who combined her Global Water Dolphin Meditation with the Marine Meditation in 1998 and has organized the Marine Meditation website as an adjunct to her own Dolphin Empowerment website ever since. Also **Kaye Ogilvie**, Intuitive Spiritual Artist, who Painted all the Labyrinths walked during the Marine Meditations, as well as many other inspirational images that have assisted my Journey of Growth.

I also acknowledge all those here in Australia and those throughout the World who have supported me and encouraged me over the years, and in particular**, Barbara Wolf and Margaret Anderson**, who's vision and hard work has made this book possible.

BLESSINGS OF LOVE, JOY AND PEACE TO EACH AND EVERY ONE OF YOU.

DAVID J ADAMS

FOREWORD

We Humans live in the concept of "Linear Time', which divides 'Time' into minutes, hours, days, months, etc. and goes in a straight line from 'Past' through 'Present' to 'Future', consequently we give importance to the date on which something happens. Our Spiritual and Cosmic Friends are not bound by such constraints, they operate in the **'Now'** moment, so although the messages within this book have 'dates' attached to them, they are, essentially, **TIMELESS**.

Some messages do, of course, refer to specific events, such as the Equinox or the Solstice, or even some man made event, however, the underlying message is always **TIMELESS**. So we ask, when you read these messages, that you accept them as having importance within the **'Now Moment'** of your lives. Although we have given the date of receipt at the end of each message, they are not in sequential 'linear time' order.

All messages were received within the Pendragon Meditation Circle and always began with the 'Sounding" of the Tibetan Bowls, the Blessings Chimes, the Drum, and occasionally other percussion instruments. Many of the messages make reference to these Sound frequencies.

Let the messages speak to your Heart, for that is what they were intended to do when they were given by **Beloved Germain**.

Blessings of Love, Peace and Joy

David J Adams

INTRODUCTION

When I was awakened to my Spiritual Journey by the Harmonic Convergence of August 1987 I was 'introduced' to Beloved Master Germain by Heather Niland, who had worked with him for quite some time. It was not, however, until January of 1991 that I received my first direct message from Germain, when he invited me to begin a Global Meditation based on the 'Consciousness of the Oceans of the World'. I have to admit that at first I thought it was a mistake and that the message was meant for Heather herself, until she smiled and said "David, don't you realize the message is for you?", as soon as she uttered those words, energy raced up and down my spine like electricity, and I realized she was right.

That began a wonderful partnership that has continued to this day. I ran the Marine Meditation for 22 years at 8pm (wherever you were in the

World) on each Equinox, until my own Moana Beach based Meditation came to an end at the September Equinox in 2012 after 44 Meditations had been held.

This was significant in that I have always worked with Beloved Germain in the vibration of the number 8, so 44 (8) meditations at 8pm on an 8 Beach, seemed appropriate. Interestingly, perhaps, Germain conducted the Meditations through me for the first 8 years from 1991, but was then joined by Masters Hilarion and Djwhal Khul for the remainder of the time.

The messages within this Book are but some of the many Messages of Love and Joy and Self Empowerment that Beloved Germain channeled through me within the Pendragon Meditation Circle, others may well follow in Part 2. Some People refer to him as Master Germain or even St. Germain, however, in the Messages he always referred to himself as **'The Germain'** as if that were a title rather than a name, but to me, I guess he will always be **'Beloved Germain'**.

I hope his words of Wisdom resonate within your Hearts and give you upliftment on your Journey of Growth.

Blessings of Love, Peace and Joy.

David J Adams
(djpadams8@tpg.com.au)

CONTENTS

1

EMBRACE 'SILLINESS' ON A DAILY BASIS

(The Circle opens with the Sounds of the Tibetan bowls and the Blessings Chimes.)

Feel the Sounds of the Blessings Chimes uplift you into your Soul Dimension, and embrace *ALL* around you with the deepest Love from within your Hearts, connecting in *ONENESS,* and focus on the centre of your High Heart, your Soul Heart and feel it begin to pulse and beat with the highest frequency of Light that exists within your Soul Dimension.

Greetings, Dear Hearts, I am the Germain - The I am that I am.

I do not think that anyone has ever accused The Germain of 'silliness' and yet tonight that is precisely what I have come to speak to you of, and even encourage you in - the ancient art of 'silliness'.

You might perceive this as a little strange, but *in reality it is the essence of 'Being'.* I draw your attention, Dear Hearts, to those young babies as they first begin to experience themselves as physical Beings, as they begin to experience the world around them. How often do you notice them making peculiar faces then bursting into giggles, throwing their arms and their legs around and bursting into giggles?

They are not doing this to entertain mothers and fathers or friends, they are doing this purely to accept the joyfulness of discovering themselves, and they do this by 'silliness', by trying different things and laughing when they achieve them, *they are opening themselves to experience ALL that is around them.*

That is 'silliness', but of course as these small babies begin to grow, they begin to take on some of the constrictions of the third Dimensional frequencies and they begin to lose that sense of joyfulness in discovering themselves. By the time they are grown into adulthood they have almost entirely lost this ability to be filled with 'silliness', and yet, Dear

Hearts, this is exactly what you need to foster in your lives, particularly at this difficult time.

As has been mentioned many times, you are going through a period of great change upon the Earth Planet, beloved Margot specifically said this was going to be a year of *'choices'* and as you look around you at your Planet, you are seeing these choices being made in different parts of the world, and in some parts the choices have come as quite a surprise, not at all what was expected, and of course that engenders fear - *fear is the enemy of 'silliness', the enemy of joyfulness.*

Humanity has never been very good at change, indeed they have never been very good at making choices either, for you see when Humans realise they have a choice to make they begin to worry, they are like a dog with a bone, they keep on gnawing, and gnawing, and gnawing at the subject and fear builds up, and then when they actually make a choice there is perhaps a moment of relief - even sometimes a moment of excitement - but then immediately afterwards they go back to worrying, about whether they've made the right choice, or the wrong choice, or what their choice is going to bring forward, and once again the fear builds up.

In some respects, Dear Hearts, this is 'silliness' personified, because you never achieve anything by worrying about it, you never achieve anything by fear, you only achieve things by opening, embracing, daring, because this is what Love is made of, this ability to make a choice, to go through change and to embrace the experiences, just like the little baby opening in this great big huge strange world and discovering itself.

When you lose this desire to experience yourself and you start looking outside of yourself for answers, you become limited in your thinking and your feeling, ***and I am here tonight to encourage you to return to that inner child and to embrace the 'silliness' that brings Joy,*** and I am sure, Dear Hearts, from time to time you do this, you may be driving along in your car and you have the radio on and a song comes on and immediately you begin to sing and move your hands around and pull funny faces and then you look out the window and you think "oops, I hope no one saw me doing that", but for just that moment, you have indulged in 'silliness' and you have released those special feelings of Joy within yourself before you quickly crush them in case somebody else notices.

Think about that, Dear Hearts, over many years now you have received messages asking you, begging you, telling you, to do things on a daily basis - to meditate for a particular period of time, to pray, to give thanks, I am asking you to ***embrace 'silliness' on a daily basis*** - when you are washing your face in the morning and you're looking in the mirror, make funny faces, make yourself laugh, let the feeling of *Joy of your Being* emerge once more, because this is the antidote to worry and to fear, and you need to balance - in these times of turmoil and change - you need to balance yourself.

Enlightenment is not about being serious, from time to time as you know, we have joked with you because we do not wish you to be serious at all times, because when you are being serious you are restricting the joyfulness within yourself and until you release this joyfulness within and until you begin to accept yourself for the joyful Being that you are, you cannot gift Love, you cannot share Love.

Love itself is not serious, Dear Hearts, it is JOY, it is UPLIFTMENT - you do not uplift your Spirit by worrying about things, by being afraid of things, those who have sought to be in charge of your lives work with fear and worry very well, and you know this, you know this right at this moment in your country with your election campaigns. People are not coming to you and opening themselves to you and allowing you to see their beauty, to see the truth within them – oh no, they are giving you worries and fears so that you don't think too much, you don't look within yourself for the truths of things.

Embrace 'silliness' on a daily basis, perhaps just for a few moments – as I said, it may be in the car when you are driving, or maybe when you are looking into the mirror, it may be when you are taking your clothes off to go to bed and you start humming that stripper song. No one else can see you, Dear Hearts, you are not doing it to make other people laugh, you are not doing it to seek approval from other people – you are doing it purely and simply to generate the essence of Joy within yourself, because the more you can bring out this Joy from within yourself the more you radiate Light.

Enlightenment is just that, Dear Hearts, it is about 'lightening up', it is not about being serious, it is not about being dedicated to a cause, it is about awakening the Light within yourself, and you do this by expressing Joy at things you discover about yourselves, and you do that through being 'silly'.

I invite you to try this, just for a few days to see if it works for you, because of course it will not work for everyone, but even amongst your Spirit friends we enjoy the 'silliness' of Being, because that is a part of Being.

You may find wisdom through books, you may find wisdom through courses, and you may feel that you are on the path to ascension because you have done all this reading and these courses, but have you found the seed of Joy within yourself, and *have you allowed that seed of Joy to germinate within your Heart and to explode out into the world?*

No, Dear Hearts, you don't have to go around smiling at everyone, telling jokes, trying to be funny, embrace the 'silliness' of being **YOU** and of discovering the inner child once more who has this sense of wonderment about what they are, who they are, discovering it every day. *Every moment of every day can be a discovery of yourself, for THAT, Dear Hearts is the true ascension - discovering and embracing the <u>EN – LIGHTEN - MENT</u> within yourself.*

I am sure this is not the talk that you thought I would come and give tonight, but there is so much fear around at the moment, there are so many concerns, there is so much uncertainty, that people need to take a moment and to relive what they once were – *simply Beings of wonderment* - finding humour, finding Joy in everything within and around them, and I ask you to do this now, to balance out the fear, to balance out the worries, ***embrace the 'silliness' within you.***

(27th June 2016)

2

THE BLESSINGS CHIMES SPEAK TO ALL OF HUMANITY

(The Circle opens with the Tibetan Bowls, and the Blessings Chimes.)

Greetings Dear Hearts, I am The Germain, The I am that I am.

It is good to hear and feel the vibrations of the Blessings Chimes ring out across your Earth Planet, carrying forth this message of Blessings to everyone upon the Earth Planet, to every Being of Light on the Earth and within the Oceans.

The Blessings Chimes themselves have a specific energy frequency that speaks to the deepest part of your Soul, uplifting you in a way no other resonance can do. It is why, Dear Hearts, you were asked to work with the Blessings Chimes in your Marine

Meditation, sending out a Blessing to the Ocean creatures that speak to your Soul.

Now, the Blessings Chimes speak to all of Humanity, reminding them of the need to feel Blessed within themselves, and to share and embrace all others with the resonance of that Blessing.

You see, Dear Hearts, ***Blessing is not a judgement***, it is not something you earn, it simply exists as a vibration upon the Earth which assists all to be uplifted. It is, if you like, another bridge to the Angelic Realms, drawing you closer and closer to the highest vibrational frequencies of yourselves, and after all, Dear Hearts, this is why you have come to the Earth at this time, to experience the depths and to reach for the heights - to journey between and through a whole variety of Dimensional Frequencies in order to find the ***ultimate*** aspect of your ***Soul Self***.

All the work that you have done upon the Earth Planet to this time has been to move ever upwards, opening all aspects of your Being to the energies of Divine Love and Divine Joy.

There are many Sounds that you have worked with over many eons of time, many have assisted in awakening different parts of your Being, different aspects of your Being, S*ounds of the voice, Sounds of the drums, Sounds of the bowls,* but of these, Dear Hearts, **the Sound of the Blessings Chimes is the most uplifting of all**. It speaks to your Higher Being, it calls to your Higher Being and it enables you to become your Higher Being, and that, of course Dear Hearts, is your journey of Ascension. It is both an individual and a collective journey, for as you move into the Higher Dimensions of yourself, you move into the *'Oneness of all that is'*, and whilst you continue to recognise your own uniqueness, you become a part of the Whole, and as you become a part of the Whole your every action, your every thought creates ripples throughout the Whole.

Your every thought changes not only yourself, but the whole of the Earth Planet, and all the Light Beings upon it. Indeed it goes beyond the Earth Planet, it changes the Universe in which you live. That is the supreme power of individuals coming together in a collective, into a 'Oneness', you begin to create a new Earth and a new Universe.

So, Dear Hearts, as you sound your Beloved Blessings Chimes, feel yourself uplifted, feel your Joyfulness radiate out and encompass <u>ALL</u> upon the Earth, and BE the Highest Being that you are, refining your frequencies as the Chimes resonate in every cell of your body.

We are all, Dear Hearts, moving through great change, and it is important that this change is based on the energies of *Love* and *Joy, <u>so Sound your Blessings Chimes to the World.</u>*

(28th April 2014)

3

DO NOT 'DE-VALUE' YOURSELF, INSTEAD, 'RE-VALUE' YOURSELF

(The Circle opens with the Sounds
of the Tibetan Bowls)

Allow the vibrations of the bowls to resonate deep within your Hearts, freeing the shadows and allowing them to float away, and let your Light shine powerfully through to share with all around you, and all across the Earth.

Greetings Dear Hearts, I am The Germain, The I am that I am.

I come tonight to speak to you of the importance of *YOU,* You as an individual, You as an integral part of the Consciousness of Humanity, You as an integral part of the Oneness, the Wholeness of the Universe.

Those last two would be impossible without the first. Everything begins with You as an individual. Without You there would be no Consciousness of Humanity, there would be no Wholeness of the Universe. ***That is the importance of YOU.***

Ahh, already I can hear your minds stepping back and saying "If I were not here, someone else would be here", but that Dear Ones is a 'cop out'. You are demeaning yourself, you are making yourself seem unworthy, when in reality you are the essence of everything. *No one else can take your place, no one else has your energy, no one else has your Light, no one else has your wisdom.*

It is time for you to embrace and accept your own importance to the *WHOLE*, to the New Earth, to Humanity. This is not about ego, this is not about running around saying "I am the greatest". It is simply about accepting that you are an essential component of the whole, and whenever you radiate your energy, when you focus your intent, you are part of creating everything around you.

Think on that a moment, Dear Ones, allow it to sink into your mind, allow it to breathe within your

Heart - the knowing, the accepting of the wondrous beauty of YOU.

I say to you, do not de-value yourselves, re-value yourselves. Accept and embrace the fullness of your Being, your importance to all that is.

It has always been the case upon the Earth Planet that self-perception, and perception of others has been dominated by numbers, and in your new world of technology, this has become increasingly so. You judge your worth now on how many 'friends' you have on Facebook, how many 'followers' you have on Twitter, and yet in reality, your 'friends' on Facebook are often, at best, acquaintances, sometimes hardly known to you at all, certainly not 'friends', and in 'the twittersphere' followers are not known to you, they are just numbers.

You look out at your 'important people', those who **seem** to be 'important' with a million 'followers', and ask "how many of those 'followers' do they actually know?, would they recognise them as they walked along the street?". **No !.** So you see Dear Ones, your importance to the Planet, to Humanity, to the Universe has nothing to do with the number of 'friends', or 'followers' that you may or may not have.

It has to do with accepting that every ounce of energy you put out creates something in your World, and if you work within your Heart, you know that 'something' that you are creating is Light and Love. You may not know how many are influenced by that Love and that Light that you radiate forth, because there are no numbers attached to it, but it is important that in your Heart, you *know* that being here at this time *Matters.* You cannot be replaced by anyone else, it is your Light, it is your Love, it is your Wisdom that is here on the Earth at this time, creating the new environment, the new frequencies, the new Harmonics of the Earth.

Yes, Dear Ones, from time to time you will read that specific numbers are required to achieve change. The number 144,000 is often quoted, and it may well be that this particular number has a vibratory frequency that allows a door to be opened, but without *YOU*, there is only one less than 144,000. You cannot know the precise numbers that sit in meditation with you at your Equinox, or at other times when meditations are called upon the Earth, you do not know how many may be involved, all that matters to you is that *YOU* are involved, that *YOU* are creating from deep within your Heart the dreams that you came to this Earth to paint upon the Planet.

So tonight, Dear Ones, I speak to you of the importance of you, not of your 'followers', not of your 'friends', but of you, and I ask you to embrace the importance of you

Do not 'de-value' yourself, instead 're-value' yourself, and know with absolute certainty that without you, nothing can be created, nothing can be the same, for no one else can gift to the Earth and to Humanity that which you have to gift - ***<u>your special Light, your special Love, the essence and the importance of YOU.</u>***

(23rd September 2013)

4

LET YOUR HEART LEAD THE WAY

(The Circle opens with the Sounds of the Tibetan Bowls and the Blessings Chimes and the Drum)

Greetings, Dear Hearts, I am the Germain, the I am that I am

All those upon the Earth are moving through a time of great transition. A transition from the time where decisions were mind based, to a time when decisions are Heart based. This will be a time of considerable confusion for Humanity - the cross over time between two radically different systems of guidance, for each individual upon the Earth.

You will not be replacing one with another, you will merely be shifting the degree to which one or the other dominates.

For many of your Earth existences, reason and logic which are of the mind, have dominated your directions, your decisions, your journeys. The energies of the Earth at this time, will gradually shift to the Heart domination, where *knowing* and *intuition* takes precedence over the reason and the logic of the past.

This does not mean that your mind becomes your enemy, it simply means that reason and logic and the guidance of the mind, merely give possibilities and options, and the final determination of direction becomes the role of *'knowing'* - **your inner knowing** - your Heart direction.

Many of you have been experiencing a movement in this direction over recent times, and this has resulted in some confusions. It is not easy to move from **reason** to **knowing.** You will find that without the direction of the Heart, the reason and the logic will begin to confuse itself.

The mind will provide you with alternatives, as it has always done, but it will be your Heart that makes the final decision. So acknowledge what is within your mind, acknowledge the possibilities created through logic and reason, but feed them now into your Heart, and ask the question of your Heart, "which of these do I ***know*** is my direction?".

You will be surprised at how easily the Heart will determine your direction, for the Heart does not work in the element of fear, whereas the mind has always taken account of those things in your life that create fear. Indeed, it has invariably sought a way forward which takes account of these fears, and in so doing, has often denied you the true beauty of the life that exists upon this place.

Your Heart will always decide through Love. It is time then to begin to practice working more closely with your Heart guidance, so when you are faced with decisions, allow your mind to create the alternatives, then ask your Heart to give you the direction of Love.

When you begin to follow the dictates of your Heart, you will find more and more of your life becomes a thing of magic, of miracles, of beauty, and you begin to shed the shadows of fear, and you embrace your true reality

When you find yourself in doubt as to what action you need to take in any situation, ask for the direction of your Heart. Your Heart is aligned with your Higher Self, and will always give you the answer that is based in Love.

> *Let your Heart lead the way in all you do, and*
> *Be the Love that you are, and*
> *Share the Light that you are.*

And so it is.

(31st October 2011)

5

EMPATHIZE - NOT SYMPATHIZE

(The Circle opens with the Sounds of the Tibetan Bowls and the Blessings Chimes)

Greetings Beloveds, I am the Germain - The I am that I am.

You have received many messages over a number of your linear years, indicating that this particular year is a year of great change for the Earth and all upon and within the Earth.

As is normal for Humanity, many of you are waiting for something dramatic to occur - perhaps something cataclysmic, for your perception of change is that it needs to be dramatic in order for you to accept it.

As we have indicated to you on many occasions, change is often very subtle in energy and in attitude. Indeed, the bulk of the changes that will be taking place in this year of 2012 are changes resulting from a change in attitude by Humanity itself.

At the beginning of this year I came to this Circle and I asked you, each and every one of you to adopt a change in your attitudes, and to *'look at the Earth through your Heart'*. I am sure that many of you have noticed changes in your lives because you have looked at your world differently than you did before – not through the logic of your mind, but through the Love in your Hearts.

More and more subtle changes are taking place upon the Earth - subtle changes of energy resulting from the additional Light that is flowing to the Earth at this time. It is creating subtle changes within the fabric of the Earth - a shifting, a moving - and within each one of you subtle changes are also taking place.

Tonight I would like to add to that subtle change of attitude of which I spoke at the beginning of this year.

It is about changing from 'sympathy' to 'empathy'. You see, Dear Ones, when you perceive something wrong on your Planet and you feel sympathy, you are in fact disconnecting yourself from what is happening. For *sympathy is a judgement*.

Tonight I am saying to you, as you perceive these things happening on your Planet, instead of feeling sympathy for those who are involved, I want you to think and feel empathy instead. For empathy places you within what is happening. It is an acceptance of the unity of all things.

Empathy is about embracing with Love, not embracing with judgement.

This small, subtle change in attitude within you will again change your perspective on the Earth. It will reinforce your acceptance of the Oneness of all that is.

You are never isolated from what is happening around you. You may not be actively participating, but in energy form you are a part of all that is happening upon your Planet.

It is imperative therefore that you feel the empathy. Let go of judgement and embrace acceptance. *Sympathy is from that lower emotional area of your spleen – empathy is from the higher areas of your Heart.*

As you move through life looking at the world through your Heart, you begin to empathise with all that is happening on your Planet.

As you empathise, you begin to 'own' the energy of all things.

You begin to become a part of 'all' that is happening on your Earth.

Events are not isolated from you, unless you choose to make them so. Just as looking at the world through your Heart instead of your mind changes the dynamics of your existence on this plane, empathising instead of sympathising has a similar effect. It changes your perspective, and as you change your perspective you change the energy field around you.

As you change the energy field around you, you begin to effect changes throughout your Planet - subtle energy changes, subtle attitudinal changes.

These are the changes we have spoken of for much of the last few years, not dramatic, but effective. *For as you change the energy on your Planet to the energy of Oneness, of Love, everything begins to change.*

Those who sit back and wait for some cataclysmic event to happen so they can look upon it and say "Ahh, that is the change that has been prophesised", will miss the subtleties of the changes that are taking place at this time.

So do not sit back and wait, become a part of the changes that are taking place, simply by changing your attitudes in a subtle way, you become a part of the change, instead of waiting for it to happen.

There is such a difference in life when you move forward in Love, and embrace the Oneness of all that is, for you begin to feel your own power once more. You are no longer isolated, you are part of the whole, and you, through the Love in your Heart, are creating the changes that are taking place – *accepting your responsibility for creating the New World, the New Earth of Love, of Light, of Harmony, and of Joy.*

So I leave you, Dear Ones, by urging you to **empathize, not sympathize**.

I bless each and every one of you with the Love in my Heart.

(30th April 2012)

6

IT IS THE LIGHT WITHIN YOUR HEART THAT CREATES THE ONENESS

(The Circle opens with the Sounds of the Tibetan bowls and the Blessings Chimes)

Feel the vibration of the bowls resonating deep within every atom of your Being. Feel the Sound vibrations activating the deep Light and Love within your Hearts, allowing them to fill every aspect of your Being with Divine Light and unconditional Love. Feel yourself vibrating with a higher frequency of unconditional Love.

Greetings Dear Hearts, I am the Germain - The I am that I am.

When you came into this world this time around, you probably spent a considerable time at what you perceived as "home", surrounded by Love - unconditional Love of family, and then in time you moved away from "home" and set out on your journey of discovery, and you found that the world outside your "home" was not entirely filled with unconditional Love, and you learned many lessons, and you changed, and you adapted, and you experienced, and you grew, and it may be that from time to time you went back "home" to visit, perhaps even to stay for awhile.

Because you had changed in your perspectives and your perceptions, and indeed in your very energy signatures, "home" was no longer the same – you felt it differently, you saw it differently, and "home" itself had moved along on a new journey. Perhaps your old room had received another coat of paint, perhaps new furniture had been placed where the old and familiar used to be, and you felt somewhat disorientated, and for a brief while you probably felt maybe that this is not "home" anymore.

If you stopped looking at the differences, looking at the changes that had taken place in "home", or in you, and allowed yourself once more to simply BE in the essence of unconditional Love, then you knew you were indeed "home" once more.

The same is happening now Dear Ones to your journey "home". Beloved Unicorn welcomed you "home" to the Dimensional Frequency of Oneness, and when you came to this Planet at the beginning of time, that was your "home" - the Dimensional Frequency of Oneness, and you grew within the unconditional Love of that "home", and then you left your "home" and began your journey of discovery, creating the duality, and you found that all was not unconditional anymore, and you journeyed further and further from "home".

At times you did not even remember what "home" looked like or felt like, you became embroiled in the daily sojourn into darkness and duality, and now that you have uplifted your Spirit once more to the vibrational frequency that allows you to go "home", many of you are finding this disorientating.

You know you are "home", but you are seeing "home" through different perspectives, different perceptions. Your own energy signature is different, and of course nothing stands still in the Universe, so the vibrational frequencies of "home" have also changed in the times that you have been away.

It is understandable Dear Hearts that for some time you may not feel entirely comfortable with being "home". So I come to you tonight to ask you not to focus on the differences that you perceive, but to focus once more on the purity of the unconditional Love that is your "home".

Your friends the Unicorns, the Angels, the Ascended Masters, all your Spiritual friends who exist in this Dimension are all part of "home", and if you embrace the oneness of all that is, you will gradually let go of your perceptions of difference, and you will find yourself filled once more with the unconditional Love, the Oneness and the Unity of all that is.

Do not be discouraged, Dear Ones, if you feel a little uncertain at this time. You have come "home", and you will once more feel the Oneness, and feel the Love. The differences you perceive will fall away and become a part of what you used to be, for you have now decided that your journey of discovery has come to an end, for what you have discovered is the Light within your Heart, and it is the Light within your Heart that creates the Oneness.

I repeat to you today what Unicorn said before – *"WELCOME HOME".*

I embrace you with deepest love – *"WELCOME HOME".*

(25th June 2012)

7

TIME

(The Circle opens with the Sounds of the Tibetan Bowls and the Blessings Chimes)

Greetings Beloveds, I am the Germain, the I am that I am.

I have come to speak to you tonight about *"TIME"*. Firstly, let me say that *Time does not exist !, It never has existed in the reality of the Cosmos.* It is a construction of Humanity. What Humanity chose to perceive as an 'advance'. In the earliest of your civilizations, people moved with the cycles of the Cosmos. In some parts of your world today, people still move with the cycles of the Cosmos, the cycles of the Moon, the cycles of the Sun and the cycles of the Earth, but this is not time ! Time as you know it is a construction purely of Humanity. I am sure it was created with the best of intentions, but as with many of the things that Humanity comes up with, it served only to enslave those it was meant to assist.

How many times have you heard people say, "If only there were more hours in the day", Well, I can quite easily make more hours in a day, Dear Hearts. Today you have 24 hours in your day, is that not so?, Well I decree that tomorrow you will have 28 ! Of course, it will mean that each of your hours tomorrow will be slightly less than the hours you have today, but you will have more hours in your day ! Will this resolve the issues of those who say "I wish there were more hours in the day" ? No, of course not Dear Hearts, because people are not really talking about 'Time', they are talking about *choices*, Choices they make in their lives, choices to *'be busy'* ! Even within your current lifetimes the construction of time as you know it, your hours, your minutes and your seconds have constrained Humanity further and further.

Do any of you remember in your early years of this lifetime how, when you were sick you were able to go to the Doctor? Nowadays when you are sick you have to make an appointment to go and see your Doctor and more often than not you can not get in to see your Doctor when you are sick !

Previously you simply went to the Doctor and sat in his waiting room until the Doctor saw you, which was usually on a first come first served basis. Now you are made to feel guilty if you do not turn up at the appointed time, even though the Doctor is certainly not working to the same time and you are always left waiting in the waiting room, is that not so?

You see, by constructing this time you have created problems, you have created control, and through control you have created guilt. You feel guilty if you do not fill this time, if you are late. These are all mechanisms for controlling Humanity !

It is time that you realize this, Dear Ones. It is time for you to begin to move away from the linear time that you have created, and move back into the Cosmic cycles, back into what I perceive and call *"HEART TIME"*.

"HEART TIME" is about doing things in the *NOW* because you *LOVE* to do things. That flies in the face of everything you are taught at this time, everything you are controlled by at this time.

There are no minutes, there are no hours, someone at some time came up with these, divided a Cosmic cycle and determined that there would be 24 hours in a day. Why 24? Why not 34? Why not 4? You see it is *artificial*, it is an *illusion* and when you bring your hours down into minutes the same thing applies. Why have you got 60 minutes in your hour? Why not 20? Why not 100? It is an Illusion, **Time is an Illusion**, but it is an illusion that has become so tightly woven into your society that you have become slaves to **"TIME"**.

When we speak of 'end times', some refer to 2012 as the 'end times'. I suggest to you that it is the **'end of time' not the end of the Earth**, **but the end of 'Time' as your Master !** It is time for each and every one of you, not just you here tonight, but you over the whole of this Planet, to begin to take back to yourself, responsibility for the choices that you make, and to stop blaming what is happening around you on a lack of time or on time itself.

I do not suggest for one moment that you throw away all your watches and clocks, you have created a civilization which to a large extent depends on these things, but each one of you within that system can begin to take control again of your lives. Begin to be more aware of the Cosmic cycles, and to structure your lives around these Cosmic cycles instead of around the illusions of minutes and hours.

EVERYTHING IN YOUR LIFE IS CHOICE. You may find excuses for your choices, you may find reasons for your choices, you may say something to this one (*David*) that "you don't have to worry about time because you do not have to work", but *that* is not the issue ! The issue is that there are always choices that you are making. If you are choosing to fill your life with work, or with any kind of activity, it is *YOUR* choice. If you choose to work 60 hours a week, something needs to give, and in many instances what gives is the balance within your self ! the balance with your community !. No one has 'time' to sit and sniff the flowers, to smile as you walk past someone, to speak to others, they are all rushing by, governed by the clock, governed by the next appointment. When you look up into the sky and you see the sun and the moon, they still go their way irrespective of how 'busy' you have made yourselves, the Cosmic cycles are still the Cosmic cycles.

As the new world of Love and Peace is created, do you wish to continue to be enslaved? That is the choice you have to make, and once again it *WILL be a CHOICE*, a choice for each and every person on this Planet. Your animals, they don't care, people argue about daylight saving, how it affects farmers, well the cow gets up and the cow lies down and the sun warms them and the night chills them. To them it makes no difference whether they are milked at 6 o'clock or 7 o'clock or 4 o'clock, because they do not understand 'time' they are simply *in the now* ! In many respects you can reclaim this in your lives if you choose.

So tonight I want you to look carefully within your own lives and determine how enslaved you have allowed yourself to become to this illusion you call *'Time'.* Is it time itself that is creating the imbalance in Humanity?, that is creating the illnesses, the disease, the stress? Would that stress be as great if you were simply following the cycles of the Cosmos, the natural elements of the Earth? Think about that, Dear Ones, embrace the reality of the cycles of the Cosmos and place your illusionary 'time' in perspective, move into your Hearts, and begin to operate your lives in *"HEART TIME"*.

"HEART TIME" is about doing that which you Love, about doing that which makes you feel balanced and happy and unstressed. Of course this

may require decisions that are difficult, but it is only a *'CHOICE'*. There is no judgment for anyone else to make as to the choices *you* make, but equally, having made those choices, there is no point in you complaining that there are not enough hours in a day, that time is speeding up. It is all an illusion !

The only thing that creates your reality is the choices you make from the moment you wake up to the moment you go to sleep. You create your reality with your choices.

It is time for each person to take personal responsibility for their lives. You are not a slave to the illusion of time. Set yourself Free, move into your Heart, into your *"HEART TIME"*

Blessings to you Dear Ones, I am the Germain, the I am that I am.

(24th May 2010)

8

YOU ARE ALL DIVINE
BEINGS OF LIGHT

(The Circle opens with the Sound of the Tibetan Bowls, the Blessings Chimes and the Drum)

Allow yourselves to flow deeply into the Divine aspects of your Being, acknowledging every Dimensional aspect of your Being, embracing the fullness of your power with deep unconditional *Love of Self.*

It is within your ***Love of Self*** that you find the ***Love of others***, for as you embrace Love of Self, you free yourself from fear and judgement, and you radiate forth the Love that acknowledges the *UNITY OF ALL.*

Greetings Beloveds, I am the Germain, the I am that I am.

I come to you this evening to awaken a special Lig within each one of you – that **Light of the Divine** that you have hidden deep within yourselves for so long, so afraid to show your Divine Light, afeared of the judgements of others.

There is no doubt over many of your lifetimes that you have faced these judgements, that you have been punished, perhaps, for daring to show your Divine Selves to others. In those times you have oft moved into different Dimensional frequencies – those frequencies that allow you to embrace and enjoy the deep Love, the deep Serenity, the deep Joy of embracing the Divine within you.

There are many places on your Planet where such journeys into other Dimensional frequencies have been well documented, and I ask you tonight to focus specifically on the Gateways to those other Dimensional frequencies – to those Sacred places such as Avalon, a Dimensional Frequency of Light where most of you have sought refuge from time to time.

The Earth itself is moving into those Sacred Dimensional Frequencies at this time. The veils that have hidden Avalon and other Sacred places from the view of Humanity are melting away.

Feel the powerful energies of these places awaken within your Hearts, the *knowing* – the comfortable *knowing* of your own *Divinity*.

Accepting and acknowledging your own Divinity does not place you above others – it allows you to embrace all others with Love, with acceptance.

Many of your Religions have sought to create the Divine as something above and beyond mere mortals. Such power will no longer be a part of your Earth, for the Divinity within each one of you will recognize the Equality of all that is, the Oneness of all that is.

Take a moment this evening to flow into the special energies of Avalon, or Shambahla, or Lemuria, or Atlantis.

Embrace the Divine within your Heart, and allow the knowledge and wisdom of other Dimensions to become open and apparent within your Hearts, and within your minds.

> ***You are all born of the same Seed – the Seed of the Creator.***
> ***You are all Divine Beings of Light.***
> ***You are all Love.***

Go with the flow of the Love Energy within you.

(David Sounds his Tibetan Bowl)

Feel the Sound Vibrations uplifting you, expanding you. Let your Love and your Joy Sound forth to embrace the Earth – to embrace the Universe.

Sound forth your Divine Love.

IT IS TIME TO WALK YOUR EARTH IN THE DIVINE LIGHT OF YOUR TRUE BEING.

It is time to Bless the Earth with Peace and Serenity, with Love and with Light – **FOR THE HIGHEST GOOD OF ALL.**

So mote it be.

(23rd May 2011)

9

ONENESS IS PERSPECTIVE

(The Circle opens with the Sounds of the Tibetan Bowl, the Blessings Chimes and the Drum)

Greetings, Dear Hearts, I am the Germain, the I am that I am

Once again we have a reaffirmation of the message of the coming together of the Divine Feminine and the Divine Masculine within each one of us, and collectively within the World as a whole. The coming into *Oneness* – a word we have used many times over the years but have yet to fully grasp and fully embrace and fully accept. We may never fully understand Oneness, because our mental faculties grapple with things we can not see, and Oneness is something we can not see, it is something we can only feel and embrace and be a part of.

So take a moment to focus on each of your Chakras individually, moving initially upwards from the Base Chakra to the Crown Chakra and above, embracing each individual Chakra, empowering each individual Chakra.

Imagine the Chakra as a wheel of Light radiating forth a beautiful colour vibration and a Sound vibration. Move slowly through each of the Chakras within your body, and then reverse the process and focus on each of the Chakras from the top to the Base, focusing on each individually.

When you have embraced and honoured each of the Chakras, allow your imagination to move away from your physical body to the point where you no longer see your Chakras as individual wheels of Light. You see them come together and become a *Oneness*, and you are able to see the full beauty of the Rainbow Light of your *Self.*

You see, individuality and Oneness are but a matter of perspective, and as you perceive yourself more and more from a Higher perspective, you begin to see the Oneness of yourself. You begin to see the fullness of your Being, the Rainbow strobes of Light radiating forth in a spiral of magnificent Light

Energy, and you begin to see yourself in the fullness of your majesty.

As you draw even further away from your Physical Body in your imagination, you begin to appreciate that your Light is intermingled with the Light of those next to you into a magnificent Oneness of radiant Light, so once again, a different perspective of your energies.

As your Light merges with the people alongside of you, you see the interaction, you see the beginning of the *Oneness of Humanity,* and the Light becomes stronger. ***ONENESS IS PERSPECTIVE.***

Now in your imagination, allow yourself to move closer, and as you do so notice the separation beginning to occur, until you are once again identifying and embracing each of your Chakras individually, *and you begin to understand that separation is simply an illusion of distance,* and that you are a part of the Oneness of all that is, if only you will allow yourself to see it.

Now, in your imagination, move even closer and allow yourself to be drawn into each of the Chakras, into its Light, into its Colour, into its Sound, and within each Chakra you will begin to see the separation of the Colours, the separation of the Sounds – again, *Perspective.*

Take a moment to take a journey through each and everyone one of your Chakras, moving within them, through them, feeling the unique vibration that each provides to your Total Being. Listen to the Sound of your own Light, Listen to the flow of energy through each of your Chakras. Listen to the melody that each proclaims as it sends forth into the World the individual Light of each chakra. Now slowly draw back until you are once again aware of each of the Chakras in front of you. Embrace their connectedness, Honour their Individuality, their Uniqueness, as part of the whole. Then draw slowly back further again until all the Chakras merge into a Oneness of Colour and Sound. ***Embrace and Honour the fullness of the Light Being that you are.*** Then, once more, move further away and see yourself, and embrace yourself as part of all that is.

All life is perspective. Allow yourself to shift your focus from one perspective to another, accepting that all are valid, but ***know*** that the Highest Perspective is the Perspective of Oneness. The perspective of Oneness allows you to fully embrace your brothers and sisters upon the Earth, and your brothers and sisters beyond the Earth, as part of your total Being.

At any time, and in any situation in your life, look always from the Highest perspective.

Know deep within your Heart that in any circumstance there is always another perspective to look at. Do not be afraid to explore and experience different perspectives of any situation or any circumstance.

Now move in your imagination deep into your Heart Chakra, and allow your innermost Sound to radiate forth. Every breath you take sets up a resonance in your physical vessel that creates a unique Sound. That Sound is amplified through each of your Chakras and radiates forth to the World you live in. You Breathe *Sound*, You Breathe *Colour.* Embrace the totality of your *BEING*.

FEEL YOUR OWN ONENESS.

*Now see yourself as a **TOTAL BEING OF LIGHT**, interacting with all around you, empowering each other with the Sound of your Being.*

Blessings of Love be within each one of us.

And so it is.

(22nd November 2010)

10

YOU ARE THE MASTERS

(The Circle opens with the Sounds of the Tibetan Bowls and the Drum)

Greetings, Dear Hearts, I am the Germain, the I am that I am.

Just relax, allow your Heart to open wide and embrace the flow of energy – the flow of energy that has moved around the Planet at this special Equinox time. The energy of Light and Love that each one of us radiated forth through the Oceans of the World, and connected with all the Light Beings of the Planet – within the Oceans, and outside the Oceans. Setting up a tapestry of Light across the Earth – a tapestry of awakening, allowing each Being to find the Love and the Light within their own Hearts.

Now feel that energy flow back into yourself, embracing you, changed and empowered by each additional fragment of Light from its journey. Welcome it home into your Hearts.

KNOW that this is the beginning of a new stage of your journey –
Your journey of discovery,
Your journey into the totality of your own Being,
The acceptance of your own Mastery,
An awakening to the *UNITY OF ALL.*

The time of being separate is over. The time of coming together in ONENESS is upon us.

As you receive the flow of energy back into your Heart, do not hold onto that energy – allow it to radiate out once more to share your Light and your Love with all the other Light Beings around the Planet, and Light Beings beyond the Planet.

It is through the coming together in Oneness that the Earth will be shifted into new Dimensional Frequencies.

Just allow yourselves to feel the energy,
Feel the Lightness of Joy,
The empowerment of Love,

And allow your Heart to speak through this wave of energy,
To all the Beings of Light, in all Dimensions –
Within and upon the Earth,
Within and upon the Oceans,
Within and upon the Stars and the Planets,
Within and upon the Sun and the Great Central Sun.

Know that you are a part of all these energies.

The wave of Love and Light you began at 8pm on the Equinox has now become empowered to continue to shift and move around the Planet, and out into the Cosmos, carrying with it new Light, new understanding, new acceptance – an acceptance based on Love and Peace.

It is a new dawn of opportunity. Become a part of the flow of that Light and Love energy, and let it grow, and grow, and grow, within you and around you.

ACCEPT THAT YOU ARE THE MASTERS – THE CO-CREATORS OF THE NEW EARTH.

Honour yourselves, so that you may in turn honour others.

Love yourselves, so that in turn you may Love others.

BE THE LIGHT YOU ARE MEANT TO BE !

(21st March 2011)

11

EVERYTHING IS IN PERFECTION

(The Gathering opens with the Sounds of the Tibetan Bowls and the Drum)

Feel the upliftment of the vibration of the Tibetan Bowls and the Drum resonating deep within your Hearts and uplifting you into your Soul Dimensions where you can gaze out upon your World and see it in *ONENESS,* and acknowledge that you are part of the *Oneness of all that is.*

Greetings, Dear Hearts, I am the Germain, the I am that I am.

Yes, I know you have been speaking of me, and I have been enjoying listening. Indeed, I have enjoyed participating in your recent *"Waters of the World Ceremony".* I hope you had fun creating and performing this powerful Ceremony, for it was intended to be a Joyful experience for each and every one of you, for when there is Joy within your Hearts you 'Light up', and as you Light up you Light up the World around you, and others will be drawn to that Light and see within it a spark of the Light within themselves, and then they too will embrace Joy.

But most of you, Dear Hearts, have been working with the Masters for long enough to know that nothing is quite as it seems on the surface, nothing is ever by accident and nothing is ever done in isolation. It is always a part of a Journey, a part of the WHOLE.

That applies particularly to your recent Ceremony, the *"Waters of the World"*. You were asked to perform for a Lunar Cycle, working with Crystals, working with Water, working with Lunar energies, and as you did this, each and every moment of each and every day of the Lunar Cycle you were connecting to the Waters of the World, and assisting the Waters of the World to embrace new vibrational frequencies of Light. This was not about the pollution in the Third Dimension, this was all about pollution in other Dimensional Frequencies that was preventing the Waters of your World from assimilating quickly and easily the new Light Frequencies coming to the Earth Planet at this time.

It was not timed accidentally, as you must have realized, the period of this Lunar Cycle encompassed the Lion's Gate, that time in your calendar when the gateway to Sirius is opened, when energy flows between the **Heart of Earth Mother** and the **Heart of Sirius**. Sirius, as you know, Dear Hearts, is a constellation, and within that constellation is Sirius B, which is the Planet of the Cetaceans, the Whales and the Dolphins - and **in particular the Golden Dolphins of Higher Frequencies**.

You will also recall that you were informed by Beloved Margot that she and Tarak were moving from the Earth Planet to Sirius through the Lion's Gate gateway, for the next work that they are required, or should I put it, asked to do, in regard to the new Frequency of energies that will be coming from Sirius in the near future. You see, all this, Dear Hearts, is tied together. Your Ceremony to assist the **"Waters of the World"** in accepting the energies that will be coming from Sirius over this next period of time between now and the time of your Equinox, through the period of the 9:9:9 energies **Everything** *is aligned, everything is connected, everything is in perfection.*

Because in your Third Dimension Physical vessels the majority of you *IS* water, you too have been accepting these new energy Frequencies, but this next inflow of Sirius energies will not be directed through Humanity as many of the flows of energy in the past few years have been directed, these energies will be directed to the Whales and the Dolphins, which is why, Dear Hearts, it was important at this time to work at clearing the energies of the Waters of the World, of the Oceans of the World, for the Whales and the Dolphins will need to absorb, accept, assimilate, these new Higher Frequency energies from the Golden Dolphins and from the Whales of Sirius, that they may *Sound* those energies into the Crystalline Grids of the Earth Planet.

Some of you may not be aware that the Whales in particular are connected powerfully with the Crystalline Grid structure of your Earth Planet, and in many instances because so much of your Earth Planet is covered by the oceans of the World, it is they who do the Sounding into the Crystalline grid structures to maintain their Balance and Harmony. Beloved Margot and Tarak were here on your Earth

Planet to work with Dylanthia to amalgamate the Songlines, the major 12 Songlines of the Earth Planet - the arteries of Earth Mother – with the Crystalline Grid structures.

You see, Dear Hearts, nothing is in isolation, everything is inter-connected, not only on and within the Earth but within the Cosmos. So as you place your newly activated Water back into the oceans, and imbibe within yourself, know that this will facilitate the inflow of the next powerful energy source from Sirius. You will feel those energies as they arrive upon the Earth Planet and you may wish to connect through your Hearts to the Whales and the Dolphins, to all the other Cetaceans, all other creatures within the oceans, within the lakes and within the rivers, *MAKE THIS A HEART CONNECTION.* For it is through them that the next step in the Ascension of the Earth Planet into a new Dimensional Frequency will take place

It is through the Sound of the Whales and the Sound of the Dolphins that Earth Mother will be uplifted totally and completely into a new vibrational Frequency of Joy. You have worked with **Love**, you have worked with **Light,** you have also worked at times with **Joy**, but this inflow is more powerful than anything you have ever experienced before in terms of the energy of *Joy.*

If you open your Hearts, Dear Ones, you will feel this inflow of *Joy* and we ask you if you feel this inflow, open your Hearts and let it *OUT FLOW* to others around you. This will be a powerful connection between you, the Whales and the Dolphins, for you are all Brothers and Sisters, you are all Cosmic Beings of Light, and you are all a part of the Heart of Earth Mother. So on behalf of the Masters of Shambhala I would like to thank you for participating in this little Ceremony with the *"Waters of the World"* and with the moon, whose energies affect the Waters of the World so greatly and yet, are so little understood. But you do not need to understand, Dear Hearts, you simply need to accept and embrace.

Reach out with your Joyful energies to all around you, but particularly reach out to the Whales and the Dolphins, give them the strength and the courage that they need at this time to further delineate the Sirius energies into the Crystalline Grids of the Earth Planet.

This is a powerful time, Dear Hearts, it is not a time to go missing, not a time to hide, but a time to **BE** what you are meant to **BE** - receivers and senders of **LOVE**, **LIGHT** and **JOY.**

Blessings be upon you, Dear Hearts.

(19th August 2016)

12

LISTEN THROUGH YOUR HEART TO THE SONGS OF THE OCEAN BEINGS OF LIGHT

(The Circle opens with the Tibetan bowls and the Tingsha bells.)

Allow yourselves to relax totally, drawing into yourself the resonance of the bowls, feeling the vibration moving through every part of your Being, Awakening and Enlightening the very essence of your Being.

Feel yourself being transported to a beautiful golden sandy beach, and the resonance of the bowls becomes the whisper of the Ocean as it speaks quietly to your Soul, reaching out and embracing every aspect of your multidimensional Being with the embrace of Love and Light - *for this is a time of coming together with the Consciousness of the Ocean.*

Feel the Love. Feel the Joy. Feel the Harmony as you find yourself merging into a state of Oneness with the Consciousness of the Ocean. Within that Consciousness greet and embrace the Light Beings of the Ocean Dimension. Embrace Beloved Whale, Beloved Dolphin, Beloved Dugong, and Beloved Turtle, for all these await you and embrace you, for this is the time of Oneness, the time of Unity.

Feel your body move gently with the waves of the Ocean, and *listen through your Heart to the Songs of the Ocean Beings of Light,* and allow your Hearts to sing back to them of the deep Peace and Harmony and Serenity that you feel - that you *are*.

Allow yourselves to flow through the Ocean Consciousness, communicating with each and every Being of Light, forging a new understanding, a new acceptance, a new Oneness with all that is.

Through your new Light Being friends within the Ocean Consciousness reach out to the Cosmos and embrace the inflow of special energies of this time of great change upon the Earth.

It is a time to let go of fear and to open your Hearts to embrace the Love and the Light of the Creator.

Hear it in your Hearts and feel it in every atom of your Being - the pulsing vibration of Love and Light flowing through you, becoming ONE within you.

Allow the upliftment of Joy to fill every part of your Being, allowing your Inner Vision to take control of your life, to understand all the wisdom that is contained within yourself, for it is time to ***Release that Wisdom,***

To ***SHARE that Wisdom,***
To ***BE that Wisdom.***

Many lifetimes you have waited for this moment, embrace it with Delight.

Open – Open – Open - for as you release the limitations within yourself you embrace all that is, all that was, and all that is to be.

I am the Germain – the I am that I am, and I am delighted that you have enjoyed my meditation once more at your last gathering, for it contained a message of great importance for this time – the message of loving yourself and creating within yourself - Healing, Light, Love and Joy that you may then share those things with others.

Release the last of the shadows that have limited your perceptions of life, and embrace the Light within yourself and shine that Light for others to find themselves in the mirror of your Being.

I look forward to being with you at the Equinox, to share once more the Oneness with the Ocean Consciousness.

Blessings be upon you.

(17th September 2012)

13

YOU CHANGE THINGS ON YOUR PLANET WITH LOVE

(The circle opens with the Sounds of the Tibetan Bowls, the Blessings Chimes and the Drum)

Embrace the Light and the Sound within this Circle tonight and absorb the energies of Love that permeate the whole of your Being and the whole of every Being within this Circle and beyond this Circle. Feel the energy of Joy erupt like a volcano within your Hearts to push away any last vestiges of darkness in your immediate vicinity. For tonight, as a Circle, we are creating a *'Ball of Light'* containing the ***Divine Love*** energies of each and every person within the Circle, and we will expand that *'Ball of Light'* until it embraces and encompasses the whole of the Earth Planet, and as it embraces the whole of the Earth Planet it attracts the **Divine Love** from the Hearts of all Beings upon the Planet, and it creates a sphere of Passion and Compassion, of Love and Light that infuses every single Heart upon the Earth Planet at this time - Human and non-Human - for **Earth Mother is calling out for Love.**

Greetings, Dear Hearts, I am the Germain, The I am that I am.

This **IS** a special time upon the Earth Planet, although to many it may seem to be a time of darkness, a time of turmoil, it is also a time when Love, Light and Peace are building powerfully throughout the world. *The Magenta Light* is coursing through the veins of all of Humanity and creating change within every individual Heart - and through every individual Heart, the collective Heart of Humanity.

The Light that you as Light Workers are casting out across the Earth is making the shadows of the past become visible to all, and when they are visible to all they can be embraced by your Love - not by your fear – BY YOUR LOVE, and the shadows of the past will melt before the power of that Love.

Take a moment now to empower the Love within your Heart and radiate it forth within that *'Ball of Light'*, feel yourself expand and embrace the Earth within your Heart.

Do not send out judgment, Dear Ones, send out only Love and allow the energies of Love to do the work of creating change upon the Earth. ***You do not change things upon your Planet with blame, with anger or with fear, <u>you change things on your Planet with Love.</u>***

You may not be able to perceive the changes that are taking place within the Hearts of others, simply know that it is happening and be prepared to embrace every opportunity to share your Love, to share your Light.

Let go of the need to judge others, let go of the hatred, let go of the discomfort you sometimes feel when faced with things you do not understand, live within the Light of Love in your Heart.

That, Dear Ones, is the greatest contribution that you as an individual and you as collective can make for the Earth itself.

You see, Dear Hearts, *Earth Mother has no hatred within her, she has only Love and Compassion for those who share what she has to offer,* and <u>that is life</u>, life for each and every one of you, a life of Love, a life of Respect, a life of Joy.

Feel yourself become **ONE** with the Heart of Earth Mother and reflect that Love, that Light, that Joy, and know deep within your Soul that this will change everything.

All the energies that have been pouring into the Earth from the Cosmos over recent times are designed to allow the Earth to grow in Love. These are not energies of destruction, these are energies of Enlightenment - not the Enlightenment of the Mind but the Enlightenment of the Heart.

The time has come to **BE** within your Heart at all times, and to live the energies of Love, to Live the energies of Peace, to Live the energies of Harmony, and to live Joyfully one with one another - Equality, Liberty.

**Sit within your Hearts and reach
out for each other and**

***CREATE THE ONENESS
AND FEEL THE JOY.***

(16th November 2015)

14

MOVE INTO THE RHYTHM
OF COSMIC TIME

(The Circle opens with the Sounds of the Tibetan Bowl and the Blessings Chimes)

Focus on your Heart Chakra, and as you focus on your Heart Chakra place into that Heart Chakra - to be bathed by your healing Light - all those who have been brought into the circle tonight for healing, and for helping to let go. Bathe them all in the energy of your Love. We ask only for what is appropriate to their highest good. We do not choose their healing, we simply give them, share with them, the Love that is within our Hearts, the Light that is within our Hearts, for **Their** highest good. Within our Hearts we let go of any expectations.

Feel the power of your Love, feel the power of your Light, radiating forth, embracing each of those people, and moving out into the World to embrace all those in need of Love, of Compassion, of Understanding. We ask only that our Love assists each and every person *for their own Highest Good*.

Greetings Beloveds, I am the Germain, the I am that I am.

I have spoken to you previously about the illusion of linear time, and about the need at this time for each and every one of you to move into the rhythm of Cosmic Time. The time that I refer to as *HEART TIME.*

You see, Dear Hearts, linear time has no relevance in the cycles of the Cosmos. The work that I have been blessed to do with each and every one of you has always been in accordance with the Cosmic Cycles of Time. We have worked together at the time of the Equinox, which is not part of your linear time – it is part of Cosmic Time.

All the work that is done with each and every one of you, and with all those enlightened Beings around the earth, is done in Cosmic Time. Although Humans need, from time to time, to have Linear

Time references, these are still illusions, they are, you might say, accidental, because everything is done within Cosmic Time.

The changes that are taking place on your Planet at this time, do so within the pattern of Cosmic Time, within the *HEART TIME*, for now it is the Heart that rules Humanity, and the Heart is not guided by linear time. No date on a calendar can be chosen except where it reflects Cosmic events. When you receive messages which point to a particular date on your calendar, you can be assured that it is a part of a Cosmic Time Cycle, a Planetary Cycle. *For we would only ask of you to work with Cosmic Time.*

You are in a state of flux upon your Planet. Nothing at this moment of time is set, or stable, it is all fluid. Your Earth will become stabilized and solid once more, balanced and in Harmony in its new Frequency of Light.

When your Hearts come together with the Hearts of all those within the Cosmos, you create the Unity of purpose.

You may wonder what you can do to assist the Earth at this time, and it is so very simple – ***Hold the Earth within your Heart. Bathe it with your Light, embrace it with your Love.***

The beauty of the Earth will be expressed according to the amount of Love and Light that Humanity, and others, surround it with and fill it with. ***You will create your paradise through the Love in your Hearts, not the vision in your mind.***

Allow Love to create the beauty that your Earth will become. Focus now on surrounding your Earth with the Love in your Heart, and see with your Inner Vision the Rainbows of Light caressing the Earth, flowing through the Earth, and Know from the very depths of your Being – ***LOVE CREATES BEAUTY.***

The Earth in the new Dimensional frequencies will be a place of beauty,

Vibrating with the energies of Love,

Vibrating with the energies of Peace,

Vibrating with the energies of Joy.

See your Earth begin to glow with colours of infinite beauty, pulsing, radiating, breathing in your Love energies, breathing out the Love energies of Gaia. Each breath empowering the upliftment of the Earth and all upon it and within it.

Let go of the shackles that have held your Love energies restrained and confined, allow them to explode from within your Hearts like a million Stars, connecting you all in the unity of purpose, painting the Earth in the vast array of colours that create Love energies within you, and within the Earth.

You have all come together at this time to be part of the upliftment of the Earth into its rightful place in the ***Harmony of the Cosmos***. Feel the Joy within you at being a part of the Earth at this time.

Feel your Spirit Friends, your Guides and Angels draw closer to you as you radiate forth your Love. Feel their presence within your Being.

FOR WE ARE ALL ONE.

We are all part of the Soul Family – the family of Light – the family of Love – the family of Earth.

David J Adams

LOVE IS THE KEY, LOVE IS THE KEY, LOVE IS THE KEY.

And so it shall be.

(15th November 2010)

15

'THE QUICKENING'

(The Circle opens with the Sounds of the Tibetan Bowl and the Blessings Chimes)

We give thanks to the Trinity of Blessings Chimes that have joined us tonight - one for the Earth, one for the Oceans, and one for the Cosmos - for we are gathering together in this place the *New Song of the Earth* and the Sound Frequencies of the Universe, blessing the Earth and all upon the Earth at this time, speaking to the Hearts of all upon the Earth, encouraging and uplifting the Light within the Heart, embracing Pure Love as a *ONENESS OF ALL THAT IS*.

Greetings, Dear Hearts, I am The Germain, The I am that I am.

I come tonight on the vibration of Sound to be with you at this special time, the time of the Earth's movement into new Sound and Light Frequencies that will be completed at the forthcoming Solstice, in your time. In *our* time it is simply *'THE QUICKENING'* and we are all delighted to be a part of it with you.

We have joined you many times in your Circle, Dear Hearts, not to lecture you, not to tell you what to do, but simply to be the mirror of your Soul, that you may see more of yourself, or see yourselves more clearly than you have ever done before, for it is how you see yourselves that creates the reality of your life. You have spent many lifetimes putting yourselves down, denying your creativeness, denying your abilities, giving away your powers to others, *but that time is over, you have determined in this lifetime on your Planet to awaken to the true greatness of yourselves, to the true majesty of your Being.*

Yes, Dear Hearts, there are still moments when you fall into doubt, and you look around and perceive others as greater than or better than, and then something happens and again you begin to see yourself as the *Masters* that you are. It may be a word, it may be a smile from someone else, it may be a comment that they make about how much you mean to their lives, but it places you back on track, and once again you begin to share your Light, to share your Love - for that is your purpose, Dear Hearts.

You came here at this time to do this very job of uplifting the whole of the Earth, through your Love and your Light, and your contribution is always much greater than you realise, and that is why, Dear Hearts, from time to time we come to your Circle to join with you, to hold up the mirror to your Soul, and to share in the Love and the Light that is at the essence of your Being.

We see your Light much more than you acknowledge your Light, but this too is changing, each one of you is beginning to accept and acknowledge that you are an integral part of what is happening upon this Planet, of what is happening within this Planet, what is happening to this Planet at this time.

The whole of the Earth Planet is coming into its own power, and <u>you</u> are a part of that power. If you withdraw your power from this process, it will hold everything up, for the Earth requires every last flicker of Light from within your Heart in order to succeed in its journey of Awakening.

So, Dear Hearts, as you move now towards your Solstice, to the next *'TIPPING POINT'* along the journey of Ascension, *stand tall within your Hearts, within your Love, within your Light and reach out and touch every other Being of Light upon the Earth and within the Earth.*

As you have been told, special energies were placed within the Earth Planet at the beginning of time and these energies are now awakening. There are Beings of Light, *Cosmic Beings of Light,* from the beginning of time who have been awaiting this time and they too are Awakening and are ready to work with you to take the Earth Planet to its next stage of its journey of Ascension.

Everything is a continuous change, there is no specific moment of time - particularly of your linear time - when everything changes, when you awake in the morning and everything is different and new, and you do not know how to deal with it or handle it.

Dear Hearts, you have been prepared through many, many lifetimes on this Planet to be an important component of the Earth's Ascension, you are all growing up and seeing yourselves and the Earth in a totally different way, but you have been prepared for this and it will not come as a surprise - ***but it will come as a delight !***

Some of the changes that are taking place at this time you have been made aware of, work with the information you have already been given, where that information resonates deep within your Hearts, for the journey ahead for each and every one of you is an individual choice, even though you are part of a collective ***Oneness.***

I wish to thank each and every one of you for the Joy you have brought ME as you have allowed me to be a part of your journey.

I rejoice in the Love and the Light that IS within PENDRAGON.

Blessings Be.

(15th December 2014)

16

WE SEE YOUR LIGHT

(The Circle opens with the Sounds of the Tibetan bowls and the drum)

Listen to the drum sounding the rhythm of your Heart, calling out to the Heart of the Earth to beat in unison with *You*, that you may come together with Mother Earth in a vibrational frequency of Joy and Love, stabilising every aspect of your Being, grounding yourselves into the Heart of Mother Earth.

Then listen to the Sound of the Tibetan bowls as they call to your Soul to rise into Higher Dimensional Frequencies of Light and you connect to the Heart of the Cosmos, you become a Bridge between the Heart of the Earth and the Heart of the Cosmos, a Bridge across which the whole of Humanity will move as the time of Ascension draws closer and closer, and it is the Light that you radiate from your Heart that will call to the rest of humanity, calling each of them to look within themselves and find the Light within, and then begin to connect themselves to the Heart of the Earth and the Heart of the Cosmos, becoming yet another Bridge between Dimensions. More and more of Humanity are awakening at this time, some may not even realise that they are awakening, they simply feel different, they begin to see the World differently and they become lighter and lighter and lighter.

Greetings Dear Hearts, I am The Germain - The I am that I am.

This is such a wonderful time upon the Earth Planet as the last vestiges of darkness are being shaken loose by the vibrational frequencies of your Light and your Sound, allowing all upon the Earth to see the truth of who they are, the reality of who they may become, and to begin that fusion into Unity and Oneness that will elevate the Earth into its true magical place in the Cosmos.

You may feel at times, Dear Hearts, that you are going nowhere, doing nothing, but in reality your every breath is changing the Earth upon which you live at this time, *every beat of your Heart shakes loose more and more of the old darkness, and as you shake it loose it evaporates in the brilliance of your Light.*

We commend you for your work, for your efforts on behalf of the Earth Planet, for you all have journeyed far and opened yourselves to so much, and you do not perceive yourselves in the true Light of who you are. *WE see your Light, we see the Love radiating from your Hearts and changing the world,* whereas you, as Humans, do not see this at all, you put yourselves down far too much, Dear Ones.

It is time to accept the Light Beings that you are, and to embrace all around you with Joy and Love, and occasionally, Dear Hearts, give thanks to yourselves for being who you are, where you are, for without your contribution the true picture of Ascension cannot be formed, cannot be seen, cannot be created.

In the time to come, in the next few months of your Earth time there will be significant changes taking place upon your Planet, your contribution to these changes can not be underestimated, your minds may not see what it is you have to do, but your Hearts will know and your Souls will guide.

So take your time, relax and allow everything that is within you to radiate forth, to encourage and enlighten others, for they will be seeing different things, feeling differently, and sorely in need of guidance and answers, and you, Dear Hearts - *the Way Showers -* are in the right place at the right time to offer the right energies and the right information to assist them to find themselves, to find their own journeys.

You are not building the roads for them to travel on, Dear Hearts; you are simply allowing them to find their own road, for each one will be different, and each one will take its own time, but without the Light and the Love and the Joy that you are able to provide, many of these souls will remain unawakened.

So, Dear Hearts, take every opportunity to be the Brightest Light that you can be, to be the most Joyful that you can be, and to be the most Loving that you can be.

(14th July 2014)

17

LET GO OF THE SHACKLES
OF YOUR MIND

(The Circle opens with the Sounds of the Tibetan Bowls and the Blessings Chimes and the Tingsha Bell)

Greetings, Dear Hearts, I am the Germain, the I am that I am

We Sound the Tibetan Bowls to resonate the Love within our Hearts out into the Earth, that we may become a part of the *'Love Avalanche'*, as well as the great *'Sounding of Love to the Earth'* tonight.

We need to realize that when we Sound Love to the Planet, we are Sounding Love to ourselves, because …

There is no more separation,
No division between us and the Planet,
No division between us and the Cosmos,
No division between us as individuals,

We simply become a Pool of Love, and a Pool of Light.

Sound is created by movement, the wind is the movement of the Cosmos. The Sounds of all the Planets within the Universe are created by their interaction with the Solar winds.

Let us perceive our own Hearts as Planets within the Cosmos, and the Sound of our Hearts is our interaction with the Solar winds, and each is unique, and yet each is a part of the whole.

For this is a time of accepting responsibility, but not believing that the responsibility entails *'ownership'*, for

We do not own the Light,
We do not own the Love,
We are simply part of its flow.

So accept responsibility

For the Love that you create within yourself,
The Light that you create within yourself,
The Love that you radiate forth from yourself, and
The Light that you radiate forth into the World.

See them both as part of the flow – Your contribution to the flow, **unconditionally given, unconditionally shared.**

You are responsible for the energies you project, whether that energy is a wave of Love from your Heart, or a thought from your mind. You are responsible.

Embrace that responsibility by sending out from within yourself only that which enhances the flow of energy through you, and around you, sending out vibrations of positive Love, sending out thoughts of Light and Joy. **Become a part of the flow, for the flow is part of your journey.**

Focus now on the deepest part of yourself, and the deepest part of the Earth, and feel them come together in Oneness, embracing in the pure energy of **Love**. And from within that core of Love in your Heart, and at the centre of the Earth, pulsate the light outwards to embrace **all**, to become a part of **all**.

Let go of the shackles of your mind, and simply **know** within your Being

That you are infinite, *and*
That the Earth is infinite, *and*
That the Light of Love within BOTH are INFINITE.

We have already begun our journey into new Dimensional Frequencies, and this will move forward with an ever quickening pace as you let go of the heaviness of your past Dimension, as you absolve yourself from all the threads that are holding you to that old Dimensional Frequency.

Feel the Solar winds lift you up like the feather, and *Move you ever upwards into the depths of your Being !*

We give thanks for the Light and the Love that we create within our Hearts and radiate forth, and we give thanks for the Light and the Love that we embrace and receive from the flow of all that is.

Let Peace, Love, Joy and Harmony fill the World.

And so it shall be.

(14TH February 2011)

18

ENERGIES OF POSSIBILITY

(The gathering opens with the Sounds of the Tibetan Bowl, the Japanese bell, the Harmony and Peace Chimes and the Drum)

Greetings. Dear Hearts, I am the Germain, the I am that I am

It is good to be back with you once again in your Sacred Space in this new year and new energies. It is, however, important, Dear Hearts, to remind you that your days and your dates and your calendars are all constructs of Humanity, and bear little relationship to the Universal time - which is *'NO TIME'*.

The Universe is about movement of energy, and this occurs in cycles, cycles that you have chosen upon your Planet to delineate as days, hours, minutes, months, years, but in reality it is simply a cycle of energy that moves into a new cycle of energy, and this is not an instant occurrence, so when you began this new calendar year of yours with the 1:1:1. and the inflow of energy, this represented a change of cycle. But because there is no instant change when cycles occur, some of you are still feeling the effects of the previous cycle of 'releasing', and you need to allow this to continue to occur even as you embrace the new ***Energies of Possibility***, the ***Frequency of the UNICORN.***

The problems, Dear Hearts, that you have with your time scales is that you cut things off as if they stop and start instantly, and of course, this is not what happens in the Universe, so you need to allow for the ebb and flow during times of change of cycle.

I am sure you are all hoping that the difficult cycle of releasing was over, but it will continue until each of you individually has released that which is no longer applicable to your journey, and this will occur at different times for different people, and you need to also accept that there is a new frequency of Light coming into the Earth Planet, and when you are ready on an individual basis to embrace this energy, you will begin to do so, and that will only occur when you have released sufficiently those energies of the past that have been holding you back from your own evolution and Ascension.

Patience is important at this time. Humans do love to have things immediately, and yet you know that things grow at their own pace. No two trees, for example, grow at the same pace, nor do they grow to the same height, or the same width, for they are all individuals, but, together they create the whole of the Earth, and this is important, if all trees grew at the same rate they would die at the same time, and there would be no more trees to replace them - you understand what I am saying. Dear Hearts?

This occurs also in Humans, even in Spiritual Humans, they need to accept and embrace their own growth cycle. It can be enhanced by the energies that are flowing into the Earth from your friends in other Dimensional Frequencies and in other Planetary Systems, but they simply provide the availability of energies, it is up to you, within your own Heart and Soul and knowing, to embrace and work with these energies when the time is right for *You*.

It is important, Dear Hearts, not to look at the person sitting next to you and judge your growth by what you see in them, and yet you do this so often.

Acknowledge the growth in the person sitting next to you, but do not judge yourself in comparison to their growth, indeed, Dear Hearts, they may have started their growth many lifetimes before you, or they may have started their growth many life times after you. So you should not compare yourself with others, you should honour the growth in others, but also honour the growth within yourself, and know that you are in the right place, at the right time, and in the right awareness of yourself, to enable you to work with the energies that are flowing to the Earth Planet at this time.

You have been alerted to the new **Frequency of the Unicorn**, and this is a much lighter energy than has been coming to the Earth Planet for the last period of time, the last cycle if you like, that does not mean it is less powerful and will have less effect on you, because energy only impacts on you as far as you allow it.

I know, Dear Hearts, some of you have looked back at this last year and have noted the difficulties you have experienced within your bodies, and have *'pointed the finger'* at the energies that were coming into the Earth Planet at this time, but I am here to remind you, Dear Hearts, the energies coming in were only part of the issue, how you absorbed those energies and what you needed to do with those energies also contributed to the effect it had on your physical vessels.

So let go of blame, Dear Hearts, and simply accept that you have absorbed the energies necessary for your growth, and when you look ahead to this *'ONE'* year, and the new *Frequency of Unicorn,* You and you alone will determine how much of this energy you absorb, and how it affects your growth and your contribution to the Planet on which you reside, for you are not here in isolation, Dear Hearts, you are here to be a part of the *whole* and to *Contribute* to the *Whole.* No one else can contribute what you have to contribute, but it will always be *your choice* how much you absorb of the energies on offer, and how you then interpret that energy within yourself, and allow that energy within yourself to create the dreams and the visions that you have for helping and assisting the Earth towards its Ascension and Humanity towards ITS Ascension.

Never lose sight of the fact that you have personal choice in everything.

So if you are expecting miracles, Dear Hearts, from this inflow of Unicorn Frequency, *think again*, because it will always be up to **You**. I hope you will think on this over the next period of time, and allow yourselves the time to balance what has been and to open yourselves to what is possible in the future.

Blessings be upon you, Dear Hearts.

(13th January 2017)

19

BE THE DIVINE CHANGE MAKER THAT YOU CAME TO THE EARTH TO BE

(The Circle opens with the Sounds of the Tibetan Bowls and the Blessings Chimes)

Greetings Beloveds, I am The Germain - The I am That I am.

It is time once again for us to come together and work with the Ocean Consciousness, to assist the Earth Planet to manifest its reality, its dream, its future, *to become the Ascended Star in the Universe.*

The journey we have taken together has been long in your linear time, and sometimes arduous, but we have walked the path together, and we have moved ever upwards, ever inwards.

The messages you receive now from your Spirit friends, speak always of the Heart, of the Divine Unconditional Love within your Heart, and the need for each and every one of you to embrace the Divine Love within your Heart as your way of life - *to resonate outwards the Divine Love through every breath.*

It is time to create the Enlightenment, and Illumination of truth within yourself. You will not do this alone, you will do this together in community, for the journey has been a journey into *Oneness,* into understanding your particular place within the *Oneness,* to begin to understand who you are, and what Light you have brought to the Earth Planet at this time, what vibration of Sound you have brought to the Planet at this time, *for both your Light and your Sound are important aspects of the Enlightenment, the Illumination of the truth of Oneness.*

You are beginning to awaken to the many Beings of Light in many Dimensions, who have worked behind the scenes to assist you on your journey.

It is time now to open your Hearts and embrace each and every one of these Beings of Light. Some have communicated with you, some are yet to do so.

Embrace them all with the deep Love within your Hearts, let go of the last vestiges of fear. *Honour and acknowledge the differences.*

Do not look for the mirror image of yourself, but embrace what is presented to you, in the knowledge that Love and Oneness are here on the Earth at this time, simply waiting for you to step through and become a part of the New Earth.

We have sat in Council together many times. You have often perceived us as being separate from you, but we have always been as *One* together in Council, together in our heartfelt Love for the Earth.

As we move into the Portal that is the Equinox, be prepared to open more, to embrace more, to radiate forth more of the Love that is deep within you, the Love that you have hidden away for eons of time. Feel it bubbling to the surface, changing your attitude to life, your attitude to others, your attitude to the Earth itself.

At the beginning of this calendar year, I came and asked each of you to look at life through your Hearts, and as you have done so, you have created wave upon wave of change across the Earth, shedding Light into the darkest recesses of your Planet, revealing to others deceptions, shadows, allowing them to see for the first time what it means to **Be Love** and to **Feel Love**, and to let go of the bondage of fear.

It may well be that on the surface you still see the darkness and the shadows, but that is because they are now more visible than ever before, and you are asked not to judge them, but simply to embrace them with the Divine Love within yourself, for *it is through the positive energies of Divine Love that you will create the change.*

The time for opposing what you do not think is good or real is passed.

The time of confrontation is passed.

The time of embracing all as **One** is here, and it is the energy of Divine Love from within yourself that will lighten the Earth more and more, and more, and the shackles of bondage will slip away.

In the Light of true Love, darkness cannot prevail.

Focus - focus now on the Light, the Love, and the Sound vibrations within yourself, and ***BE the Divine change maker that you came to the Earth to be.***

As we gather around the Earth at the Equinox, and embrace the Consciousness of the Oceans of the Planet. Let your Divine Love radiate forth more powerfully than ever before, and the Ocean Consciousness will accept your Love and allow it to flow across the surface of the Earth, touching every corner.

That is what I asked you to do so many years ago. Now it is time to manifest that - to embrace the partnership of Love with the rest of Humanity, and all the Beings of Love and Light that are waiting to work with you, to be with you, to become *ONE* with you.

Beloveds, this is time of great joy, a time of great happiness.

I bless you.

(12th March 2012)

20

THE LIGHT OF DIVINE LOVE IS THE MOST POWERFUL ENERGY OF THE COSMOS

(The Circle opens with the Sounds of the Tibetan Bowls and the Blessings Chimes)

Greetings, Dear Hearts, I am the Germain, the I am that I am

Embrace the Light deep within your Being, and allow that Light to expand and explode outwards through your Being and out into the World – ***unrestricted, unlimited*** – a radiation of Pure Love.

Let go of all Judgements, of all limitations, simply embrace the Pure Light of Love within You, and radiate it forth.

Imagine your Light moving ever outwards across the Earth, and out into the Cosmos, becoming a magnet for all Light of similar vibration – *the vibration of Divine Unconditional Love* – and as you radiate forth, you begin to receive in greater measure the like vibrations from others, from other Beings, from other Civilizations, from other Planets, from other Universes, for the Light of Divine Love is the most powerful energy of the Cosmos.

As you reside within the energy of Divine Love, you begin to create Worlds of beauty, Worlds of miracles, Worlds of Magic – FOR LOVE IS THE KEY. Feel with every beat of your Heart, more and more of your Divine Love pulsating outwards, lighting the shadows of the Earth. Feel that Light reflected back to you, uplifting you, embracing you.

The time of Illusion is fading with the shadows. The time of Truth is revealed by Divine Love. Let Love be your reality. Let Love be your breath. Let Love be your vibration.

There are many *Beings of Light* awakening at this time, awakening from ignorance, awakening from suspended animation from times and civilizations past, awakening in order that we also may awaken and begin to move purposefully along the pathway of transformation and enlightenment, to embrace once more our own ***Inner Vision of 'SOURCE'***.

Feel the power of your Love now, feel yourself expanding, feel yourself becoming the Divine Light of Love that you are, and have always been.

Let your Sound flow through the Universe – the Sound of Love – the Sound of awakening.

We give thanks for the Light within Pendragon, and the Love that is radiated forth to Light the Earth, and Light the Cosmos.

And so it is.

(10th January 2011)

21

THERE IS SOMETHING NEW AFOOT IN YOUR WORLD

(The Circle opens with the Sounds of the Tibetan bowls.)

Greetings Dear Hearts, I am The Germain - The I am that I am.

I appreciate your humour and enjoy the energies of Love that permeate through each and every one of you.

We have been together for quite some time, working, playing, enjoying, learning, each one teaching the other, and yet it is but a moment in Cosmic time, and everything feels new again. Have you felt this Dear Ones? this newness, this sense of upliftment, of excitement as if you are opening a door to a new world and seeing *yourselves* for the first time, in all your majestic energy?

It is part of the energy of Joy that you have unleashed upon the Earth by accessing the Pyramids of Joy. The very fabric of the Earth Planet has absorbed these energies of **PURE JOY,** and each of you are feeling this Joy, perhaps not in every moment of your existence, but I'm sure that if you sit for a moment and simply **FEEL your own energy, you will embrace a sense of Joy.**

It is something unlike you have ever felt before, you are more in control of your emotions, you are less affected by the day to day events of your world, for you do not just *see* these events any more, you *embrace* them with this new energy of Joy, and as you embrace them they *change* in their nature - their energy structure - they become less dark and foreboding, they begin to become lighter and lighter, and they no longer drag your energies down to the extent that they did before. Have you noticed this Dear Ones? Have you *felt* it?

Ahh, this will continue to grow in the days ahead, in the weeks ahead, in the months ahead, you will feel yourselves more and more uplifted in Spirit, and as you are, you will begin to create a new Lighter world around you, and others will begin to sense the change of energy. They may not understand why they are suddenly feeling more Joyful, they may put it down to simply being Christmas time, mmmm ? but then as you well know Christmas time is not always a time of great Joy, it is often a time of conflict when expectations overcome people. So they will realise, as Christmas comes and goes, and the Joy remains, *__that there is something new afoot in your world__*, a greater sense of upliftment, a greater awareness within each living Being, of the beauty and the magic within all others.

At this particular time you are being reminded through the passing of the one called *'Mandela'* of the need for equality amongst *all*, the need for setting aside the past, for letting go of old enmities, for feeling Love for all your brothers and sisters upon this Earth, embracing each and every one as if they are yourself, no more bitterness, no rancour for perceived injustices of the past. *HE SPOKE OF THAT !!*, of letting go of bitterness, of moving forward with a new purpose of Unity and Harmony. His passing at this time simply sheds the Light once more upon the specialness of people who let go of enmity and embrace Love in their Hearts.

Feel the Joy, and do not be afraid to express that Joy to those you meet, and to those you simply are aware of without necessarily meeting, for you do not need to be face to face with another Being in order to be able to Love them, ***unconditionally***, to be able to embrace them with your new energy of Joy, to share ***freely*** the new Earth frequencies of which you are a part.

We have much to do together in the days and months to come, to empower these energies of Joy across the Earth, to share the Peace and the Love within your Hearts, to embrace ***All as One***, and do not think, Dear Ones, purely of other Beings, Human Beings, but think also and embrace also all other Light Beings on and within the Earth, Beings known and Beings unknown, ***all*** will be feeling the Joy that is permeating throughout the Earth, as each and every one of the Pyramids of Joy are opened and awakened, and share this very special energy, an energy that lifts you beyond yourself, and allows you to become the fullness of yourself.

The Crystals of the Earth are embracing and empowering and sharing these beautiful energies of Joy, and the whole of your Earth is now pulsing with a new frequency of Light, a new colour vibration, and your Hearts are irradiated with this new colour of Joy.

I wish to thank each and every one of you for working with us, sharing with us.

We embrace you all with complete Joy.

(9th December 2013)

22

'UNIVERSAL SONG OF LIGHT'

(The Circle opens with the Sounds of the Tibetan bowls, the Blessings Chimes and the bell.)

Allow your minds to be still, and within that stillness embrace the beat of your own Heart. Imagine yourself once more drawn into the Shambhala of Earth Mother's Heart, for this is a time of reconnection with your source within the Earth, and when you allow your Heart to become *One* with the Heart of Earth Mother you feel the power of unity and oneness, and you feel yourself expanding and becoming *One* with *'all that is'*, for *'all that is'* exists within *You* as *You* exist within Earth Mother's Heart.

Greetings, Dear Hearts, I am The Germain, The I am that I am.

I am so delighted to be with you once more as we move towards the equinox, the time when you and I have worked together so well for many of your Earth years, and once more I will be working with you at the time of the upcoming equinox, for ***I will be the bridge, the 'Rainbow bridge' between the Heart of Earth Mother and the Heart of the Ocean Sounders,*** for each of the Ocean Sounders is willing and able to participate most strongly in the powerful activation of the new ***<u>Universal Song of Light.</u>***

They have volunteered as you are now volunteering, for remember, Dear Hearts, you continue to exist in the Dimension of free will, but now you are reconnecting with the Heart of Earth Mother and your free will is expanding to encompass the needs, the wishes and the desires of Earth Mother.

From the beginning of time Beings of Light have existed upon and within the Earth. Each generation, you might say, of Beings of Light have sought to assist the Earth Planet to reach its rightful place within the Universe. On many occasions they have come close to achieving this purpose, but subsequent events have drawn them back into the mire of density.

This, Dear Hearts, is by far the most powerful move forward for the Earth Planet, *for Earth Mother herself has reawakened to HER true purpose within the cosmos.* In times past there has been a dis-connect between those upon the surface of the Earth and Earth Mother herself, that dis-connect has now changed and there is a new state of Oneness and unity forming vibrantly between those upon the surface of the Earth and those within the surface of the Earth, and Earth Mother's Heart.

Emotion has been removed as a barrier to the Heart expansion of Earth Mother and indeed of Light Beings upon the Planet. A sense of increasing Oneness is taking place all across the Earth Planet. Many groups like this Circle here are awakening to their connection in Oneness to beloved Earth Mother.

Many in the past - as was indicated by beloved Tarak in the message of last week - placed themselves in 'suspended animation' within the Earth to enable them to be a part of the *ultimate expansion and Ascension of the Earth Planet into its true glory,* for they have energies, they have wisdom which will be required to ensure that this time there will be no retreat from Ascension, there will be no falling back into the old energies of separation and duality.

We have all worked for eons of time for this moment, ***Feel it***, ***feel it deep within your Heart as an excitement, as a feeling of empowerment, as a feeling of total unity of purpose.***

You may spend as much time as you like in the Shambhala within Earth Mother's Heart for that is where you belong, that is where you began, and that is where you will always be, for *each one of you within this Circle has chosen to make a contract with beloved Earth Mother to be of service to Humanity, to be of service to the Earth, to be of service to ALL.*

So at the time of the equinox, Dear Hearts, you will all gather in different parts of your world, we will **all** gather, and we will **all** open our Hearts and we will **all** sing the *'Universal Song of Light'*, not a song as songs are seen upon your Planet, but *simply a vibrational frequency of Light that will empower all with LOVE,* and every Being upon the Earth and within the Earth, within the oceans, will create this vibrational frequency that will enable Earth Mother to open her Heart completely and shine her Light of Love out into the Cosmos as a ***BEACON OF HOPE*** for all the Cosmos to see, and you, Dear Hearts will be a part of that, an important part of that.

So take the time between now and the equinox to sit within Shambhala and simply *BE the beat of your Heart*, for that is all that is required, to *BE the beat of your Heart within the Heart of Earth Mother, for the beat of your Heart is the frequency of Light that will be needed.*

Allow yourself to connect with others across the globe and with your ocean Sounder friends and simply allow yourselves to be the ***HEART BEAT OF LIGHT.***

(7th March 2016)

23

ACCEPTANCE OR UNDERSTANDING

(The Circle opens with the Sounds of the Tibetan Bowl and the Blessings Chimes)

Pose the question to your Heart and to your mind, "What changes have you felt within yourselves this year, and perhaps the last few years ? Are you moving closer to your Hearts? are you moving closer to awakening the acceptance within yourself from the energies that are flowing into the Planet? or is your mind still demanding understanding before you can accept?".

That is the conundrum, which comes first, the chicken or the egg? *Do you need to understand in order to accept? Or do you need to accept in order to understand?*

The energies that are flowing into the Earth at this time are asking us to *Accept* who we are, what we are, and not necessarily seek to have a mental understanding of all things. So pose that question to yourself now – *"Am I seeking understanding, or am I seeking acceptance?"*.

Take that question into your Heart, invite your Heart to embrace it, to expand within that question, for the way you answer that question dictates the extent to which you will embrace the energies of change.

For many lifetimes you have been governed by the need to 'understand', and yet within that there has always been an 'acceptance' that is beyond 'understanding'. Some call it 'Faith' or a 'belief' – which is often irrational, has no logical explanation, and yet you still hold to that Faith or belief. That has only been a small part of your lives, but the energies of 2010 are inviting you to make it the largest part of your lives, perhaps even the whole of your lives.

You begin by *Accepting Yourself !* by accepting the fullness of your own Power and your own Light, not allowing that to be diminished by the opinions of others – for you no longer seek the opinion of others – you simply embrace the acceptance of your own Light, the acceptance of your own Power, the Power to change that which is around you simply by radiating your **Inner Light**.

As you move forward each day, you are receiving more and more vibrational energies from the Great Central Sun. You are being asked to absorb and embrace this powerful Light and to connect your individual Light with that of others to create a new Light upon this Earth, a **Light of Peace**, a **Light of Love**, a **Light of Unity**.

Allow your Hearts to expand and embrace these energies, invite your minds to work with this new **'acceptance of self'** and to plan new ways of expressing and embracing the new Light within yourself. This will be a time of great creativity, a time of great change. You need to approach this time with **Love**, with **Joy**, and with the desire and intent to create a more Loving and Peaceful existence for yourselves and for all upon this Planet.

Move deeper and deeper into your Heart, and notice that as you move deeper, the Light becomes brighter, for as you move deeper into your Heart you begin to expand yourself more and more, and you embrace more and more Light. You embrace so much Light that there is no place for the shadows of fear that have lingered for eons of time.

Feel every aspect of your Being start to vibrate with a new frequency, Hear the Sound of greater Light Frequencies. Feel them resonate within every cell of your Being. Feel each and every one of these cells expanding individually and collectively, Just as you as Human Beings need to expand individually and collectively in order to maximize the opportunities for change for the *Highest good of ALL.*

Draw into yourself now the powerful energies of the Great Central Sun. Feel yourself become a part of the Cosmic Winds, shifting, moving, becoming *One* with all the Planets, with all the Stars, with all the Suns in the Cosmos, and feel the energy of *Bliss* take root in your Heart, and begin to fly, begin to expand, begin to *Become the Sun within Yourself.*

The power of the sun is within each one of you. *Allow your Sun to shine, to radiate forth, Blessing all those you meet on your Journey*

You are in the process of creating a new beginning, a beginning based on Love and Peace.

Feel that energy of Love and Peace form and solidify within your Heart, knowing that this is the starting point of a new journey.

Let your Hearts sing with the power of the *Light* within you, sing with your acceptance of the power of yourself, sing with your determination to *Be the Light for the Highest Good of ALL.*

We are all Masters of Creation. We create the Light within our Hearts. We are sculptors of the future. We sculpt with the Light within our Hearts. We are all architects of time, and we create time with the Light within our hearts.

LET YOUR HEARTS SHINE BRIGHT.

Do not diminish your Light with the power of your mind !, *Enhance your mind with the Power of your Heart Light !*

Now is the time to look ahead and create the new Earth of *Peace* and *Love.*

So ask your Heart again …. ***"Do you accept the full power of your own Being ? or do you still need to understand before you can accept?"***

(6th September 2010)

24

RIDE THE RAINBOWS
THROUGH THE COSMOS

(The Circle opens with the Sounds of the Tibetan Bowls and the Drum and the Blessings Chimes)

Greetings, Dear Hearts, I am the Germain, the I am that I am

Focus deep within your Heart Chakra and embrace the energy of Divine Love within yourself. As you embrace the Divine Love energy allow it to express itself through you as ***Radiant Rainbow Light***.

Allow that Light to flow from deep within your Heart out into this room, out into this area, out into this Country, out into the World. Know deep within you that your individual unique Light touches and embraces everyone and everything upon this Planet, for you are much more powerful than your mind imagines.

You are a Fountain of Divine Love, a Fountain of Rainbow Light, and your Light shines not only in this Dimension, but within other Dimensions also.

Your Personal unique Light shines through many Dimensional Frequencies, and can be seen and identified by Beings within those Dimensions. So allow your Love to embrace all that is.

Now open your Inner Eyes and look around at the Divine Love Light shining from Beings in all Dimensions, reaching back to embrace you, for we are all a part of a collective beacon of Light that radiates throughout the Cosmos.

With your *'Inner Eye'*, recognize and identify members of your own Soul Family and your own Human Family that have moved to other Dimensional frequencies.

Reach out and embrace them with your Love.

Empower each other with your Light.

Allow your Rainbows to intermingle and become **Oneness**.

Through your Inner Vision embrace the innermost parts of the Earth itself – to the Beings of Light that are within that Dimension – the Inner Dimension – the Dimension of Nature Spirits – the Faery World.

Take note that Doorways that formerly held you from these areas are now open to the Divine Love within your Heart. *You can reach between Dimensions – connect between Dimensions.* Move through your Light to the innermost parts of the Earth.

Embrace the Light of the **Lemurians** that exist within the innermost parts of the Earth, and those from **Atlantis** who also continue to exist in the **'Other'** Dimensional frequencies of this Earth.

Let go of everything except the Divine Love within your Heart and you will see magnificent Light, and feel magnificent Love from all those in other Dimensions. **We are all One**.

Embrace your friends, embrace your Soul Brothers and Sisters. **Feel the Unity.**

Focus on the totality of your Being, and on your journey of discovery, your journey of Ascension. **Ride the Rainbows through the Cosmos.** Embrace the Light of Home within your Hearts.

Within the Light of Divine Love within your Hearts there are no shadows, there is no fear. There is only Divine Love.

Let the Love within your Heart light the pathway ahead for the whole of Humanity, and give strength and support to those with particular tasks in times ahead – to all those who are working for the ascension of Humanity and the ascension of the Earth.

Sound forth your Joy.

Allow your Rainbows of Light to embrace all those that have moved on at this time - for we remain ONE.

And so it is.

(6th December 2010)

25

FORGIVENESS IS NOT A JUDGEMENT, IT IS AN ACCEPTANCE

(The Circle opens with the Sounds of the Tibetan Bowls and the Blessings Chimes)

Greetings, Dear Hearts, I am the Germain, the I am that I am.

Wrap yourself in the energy of forgiveness, because forgiveness - as Love, Peace and Joy - IS an energy, so it is something you can draw into yourselves, and work with inside yourselves. You need to start to embrace forgiveness as an energy of change, because that is exactly what it is, it is an energy of change, an energy of transformation.

You tend to look upon forgiveness as simply a word that has attracted to it actual negative energies from the past. You see it, perhaps, in religious terms, you see it in relation to evil, to judgement. If you start embracing forgiveness as an energy with which you work within yourselves, this is going to manifest change within your lives much quicker. Because forgiveness then becomes something that is not simply related to actual events, it becomes an energy of transformation within yourselves.

The first impact of transforming transformational energy within yourselves is the transformation of *yourself*. This is why we speak of forgiving yourselves. Do not look at forgiving yourselves for happenings and events in your lives, you cannot go back and change those things, all you can change is how you now react to those events and happenings, so you are working with an energy that transforms yourself internally. You are looking - through forgiveness -, to transform yourselves into a more Loving, Joyful, Peaceful Being. You do not do that by reliving the events of your past, individual or even collective.

You work with the energy of forgiveness within yourself, and what you are forgiving yourself for, is *holding yourself back from your own Light !* Think about that a moment. When you hold onto things like anger, resentment, fear, guilt, you are

holding yourself back from your own Light ! **That** is what needs to be worked on through the energy of forgiveness. You are releasing yourself from the bondage of judgement of yourself ! Releasing yourself from the bondage of judgement of yourself !

Humans react to events that happen in their lives, holding on to how you reacted to that event prevents you from experiencing the full power of your Divine Being. So if you are looking to work with the energy of forgiveness within yourself, focus completely on forgiving yourself for holding back ! Once you do that, you begin to let go, and you start to embrace the true power of your own Being, your own Light. Remember the quotation from Mandela used at the recent Marine meditation **"Your fear is not of the darkness, it is the fear of the power of your own Light".** In this time of transition, it is important to let go of all barriers you have built in this lifetime and in past lifetimes that do not allow you to access the true Light of your Being. Feel that energy in your Heart right now, the energy of Forgiveness.

Forgiveness is not a judgement, it is an acceptance ! Are you ready to accept yourself as the true Being of Light that you are intended to be ? if you are, then embrace the energy of forgiveness.

Do not focus that energy on any particular incident or event, simply embrace the energy of forgiveness and allow your Light to begin shining powerfully, and feel the Love and the Joy begin to fill your whole Being. You are no longer holding back, you are no longer holding on to old emotions, old perceived hurts, you are embracing the Light of your True Being.

Forgiveness is an energy of transformation. It deals only within yourself. It has no relevance to that which is outside of yourself. ***Forgiving others by its very nature apportions blame to others. You don't have that right !*** So forgiveness can only be within yourselves.

Forgiveness is your connection to Source, the ***Allowance*** of your Light to shine fully.

Feel the power of that transformation, feel yourself expand to encompass the full measure of Light that is within your Heart.

Let go of all that is not Light within yourself.

Feel the power of Love, of Harmony, of Peace, flooding every part of your Being, every Dimension of your Being.

Forgiveness is the energy of Transformation. It is only through forgiveness of yourself that you find the acceptance of others.

I repeat, It is only through the forgiveness of yourself, that you find the acceptance of others.

It is only through the Light in yourself, that you find acceptance of the Light in others.

I am the Germain. The I am that I am. Blessings to all.

(5th October, 2009)

26

THE ACCUMULATION OF POSSESSIONS HAS BECOME A DISEASE

(The circle opens with the Sounds of the Tibetan Bowls, the Drum and the Tingsha bells)

Allow the Sound vibrations to uplift you in Spirit, feel the whole of your Being raising up in frequency, floating upon the Sound Waves as you move into your Soul Dimension, bringing together your Heart and your mind into the embrace of your Soul journey, and imagine yourself sitting upon a cloud, high above the Earth, looking down and sharing the deep Love within you with *all* upon the Earth.

Feel and see the new Light Frequencies embracing the Earth, and feel your connection to *all that is*. Feel your connection to every other Being upon the Earth Planet. Feel the *Oneness*, and allow the Joy within yourself to flow on those waves of Sounds to connect with the energies of Joy within each Being upon the Earth, for indeed, within each Being there is the energy of Joy waiting to be awakened, and you awaken the energies of Joy with the radiance of your Love.

As the energies begin to radiate within each Being, and from each Being, you change the colour of the Earth, you change the Vibrational Frequencies of the Earth, you lift everything and everyone into a heightened state of awareness – *an awareness of UNITY.*

The shadows of separation are fading fast as the energies of Love and Joy push them out of the Earth, and bring in the Light of Peace.

Greeting, Dear Hearts, I am the Germain, the I am that I am.

We have spent considerable time gathering your friends – the Ascended Masters,the Angels – endeavoring to work out how *WE*, as a group, can assist the Earth as it speeds towards its new *'Stardom'* in the Universe, and it all comes back to each one of you on an individual basis – for the ***Oneness*** of ***ALL*** is contained within the ***Oneness*** of ***You !***

You are no longer a separate entity, you are an essential part of the whole, and it is time for each one of you to take stock of your lives, to look at your perceptions, to look at your preconceived ideas, to determine which of these is appropriate for the New Earth Frequencies

Over the last few years you have each done some considerable clearing and cleansing of old energies, but there is still more that needs to be done. You continue to exist in a Dimension of 'form', a 'Material' Dimension, and within this Dimension you have become accustomed to perceiving, and even identifying your 'self worth' with the Material possessions that you have accumulated.

Indeed, in much of your lives you have drawn these material possessions to you purely and simply to enhance the way you appear to others. It is time, Dear Ones, to let go of that perception, to let go of that reasoning, and to look upon the material aspects of your Dimension on the basis of what you need in order to create the pathway ahead, for you !

Some of you have already begun to let go of possessions that you realize are no longer necessary for your journey - and indeed, may be an encumbrance – so in this time of awaiting the next step of your journey, it would be appropriate to take stock of your life, to take stock of the material possessions that surround you, and to perceive each one in terms of how much Joy it brings into your life, for *that*, in reality, Dear Hearts, is the determining factor. What is it in your life that assists in creating the energy of Joy?

Any of your material possessions that do not create Joy within your lives, it is time to let them go, for those material possessions may create Joy in other people's lives, but in yours, they are an encumbrance ! they are weighing you down ! preventing you from becoming free, alive, prepared for the next step of your journey.

It is time to take stock once more of that which is necessary to enhance your journey, and that which is not ! Sometimes this can be very difficult for Humans, you are so accustomed to being judged by what you own or what you possess. *It is time NOW to be judged for who you are, for the Light that you shine, for the Love that you share.* Whether you are driving an old car or a super duper car, it is not relevant to your self worth, it is only relevant to how others perceive you.

The accumulation of possessions has become a disease, a disease based in 'greed', the more you have the greater your worth in the eyes of others – but is this really so?

The new age frequencies are about your *'Spiritual Selves'*, not your material selves, and although you will continue to have material possessions – because you will continue to live in a material world – it is how they become a part of you that is important.

So, I come to you tonight to ask you to take some time, and take stock of the possessions you have accumulated, and ask yourself with each and every one of them, ***"Does this still bring me JOY?"***. For the time of being judged by others, and taking your self worth from that judgement must come to an end ! Your own self worth comes from your *Love of yourself* – and you do not need possessions in order to Love yourself !

There are many changes taking place upon the Earth, and many more to come, and some of these may seem difficult, but they are necessary for you to fully let go of the old paradigms, the old rules, the old dogma.

So, go within yourselves and sift through everything in your life, and ***hold on to that which brings you JOY, and let go of that which has simply become 'a possession'.***

(4th February 2013)

GLOSSARY

Ascended Masters - Spiritually Enlightened Beings who have previously incarnated in Human form on the Earth but who are now in Higher Dimensional Frequencies.

Shambhala - A 'City of Light' in Higher Dimensional frequencies where Spiritual and Cosmic Beings work together in Oneness. Some perceive it to be situated Energetically above the Wesak Valley in Tibet. Channeled information given to me indicates that Shambhala is a structure within the Etheric comprised of 6 energy Pyramids of the 4 sided variety, connected together to form the Sacred Geometric shape of a Merkaba.

Pendragon – When David J Adams moved house in 2006 he was told in a dream that the House would be called 'Pendragon', so from that time his Meditation Circle became known as Pendragon Meditation Circle. Pendragon, of course, was the Name given to

Welsh Kings of old like Uther Pendragon (father of Arthur of the Round Table), so could be a reflection of David's Welsh heritage.

Blessings Chimes – A hand held instrument created from wind Chimes which are used to Bless the Earth, the Oceans and all Beings of Light upon the Earth.

Crystalline Grid – A structured network of Crystals throughout the Earth that are part of the electromagnetic composition of the Earth.

Songlines – there are 12 major songlines throughout the Earth which come together at two places, Sundown Hill just outside Broken Hill in Australia (they are represented here by Sculptures) and Machu Picchu in Peru. They are vibrational, or Sound Arteries of the Planet.

Equinox - An **equinox** is commonly regarded as the moment when the plane of Earth's equator passes through the center of the Sun's disk, which occurs twice each year, around 20 March and 23 September. In other words, it is the point in which the center of the visible sun is directly over the equator.

Solstice - A **solstice** is an event occurring when the Sun appears to reach its most northerly or southerly excursion relative to the celestial equator on the celestial sphere. Two solstices occur annually, on about 21 June and 21 December. The seasons of the year are directly connected to both the solstices and the equinoxes.

Marine Meditation – This was a Global Meditation initiated by Beloved Germain to be held at 8pm on each Equinox, wherever people were in the world. It focused on connecting with the ***CONSCIOUSNESS OF THE OCEANS***. It ran from March 1991 to September 2012 - 22 years and 44 meditations in all. See http://www.dolphinempowerment.com/MarineMeditation.htm

Isle of Avalon – A sacred Site at Glastonbury in the United Kingdom. The Glastonbury Tor is the remnant of this Island that housed the Divine Feminine aspects of the 'old Earth' religions. It continues to exist, but in another Dimensional form and is a 'gateway' to other Dimensions. It is also regarded as the ***HEART CHAKRA*** of the Earth Planet.

Lion's Gate - Every year on August 8th, there is a cosmic alignment called "the Lions Gate". The Lions Gate is when Earth aligns with the Galactic Center, (27 degrees Sagittarius) and the star Sirius, opening a cosmic portal between the physical and spiritual realms.

Chakra - The term chakra is Sanskrit for "wheel". Chakras are regularly depicted as spinning, colored wheels of energy. Chakras, by definition, are energy centers within the human body that help to regulate all its processes, from organ function to the immune system and emotions. Nine major chakras are positioned throughout your body, from the base of your spine to the crown of your head. Each chakra has its own vibrational frequency and color,

Lemuria - Lemuria, or Mu, was reputed to be a continent that was located in the Pacific Ocean area or the Pacific Ring of Fire. The Ancient Lemurian Civilisation stretched across the land of Mu which eventually sunk beneath the Ocean, but Lemurians are reputed by some to continue to exist and function in select places such as the Telos beneath Mt Shasta and the Temple of the Divine Feminine beneath the Andes at Balmaceda in Chile.

Atlantis – Reputed to be an Ancient and highly evolved Civilization located in the Atlantic Ocean around the area of Central America. As with

Lemuria it was reputed to have been destroyed and sunk beneath the Ocean.

Marine Meditation Light Explosion – (Front cover Picture). At the Final Moana Beach Marine Meditation in September of 2012, **Kath Smith** took many photographs of the evening on her Digital Camera. When the pictures were downloaded we were amazed to find, sprinkled through the many 'normal' pictures, some that showed massive Light Explosions from those gathered together. We were later 'told' by The Masters of Shambhala that those pictures revealed to our eyes that which we don't normally see, and that is the actual *LIGHT* that we were creating during the Meditation, and sharing with the World and the Oceans of the World.

LOVE is the KEY – (Book Title) This is the title of a song written, performed and recorded by David J Adams, and can be heard – and downloaded free of charge – at https://soundcloud.com/david-j-adams/love-is-the-key

SONGLINES – *NAMES AND APPROXIMATE ROUTES*

We have given names to the 12 Songlines that embrace the Earth Planet based on the names of the 12 Sculpture on Sundown Hill, just outside Broken Hill in New South Wales, Australia. Below we give the approximate routes that the Songlines take between Sundown Hill and Machu Picchu as they were given to us in meditation.

RAINBOW SERPENT: Sundown Hill – Willow Springs – Mount Gee (Arkaroola) – Kings Canyon (near Uluru) – Mount Kailash (Tibet) – Russia – North Pole – via the North American Spine to Machu Picchu.

MOTHERHOOD: Sundown Hill – India – South Africa – follows the Nile River to North Africa – Machu Picchu.

THE BRIDE: Sundown Hill – Pacific Rim of Fire – Machu Picchu.

MOON GODDESS: Sundown Hill – Across the Nullabor to Perth – Madagascar – Mount Kilimanjaro – Egypt (Hathor Temple) – Via the Mary Line to the United Kingdom – Machu Picchu.

BAJA EL SOL JAGUAR (UNDER THE JAGUAR SUN): Sundown Hill – Grose Valley (New South Wales) – New Zealand – Chile – Via the Spine of South America (Andes) – Machu Picchu.

ANGELS OF SUN AND MOON: Sundown Hill – Willow Springs - Curramulka (Yorke Peninsular of South Australia) – Edithburgh (also Yorke Peninsular of South Australia) - Kangaroo Island – Mount Gambier - Tasmania – South Pole - Machu Picchu.

A PRESENT TO FRED HOLLOWS IN THE AFTERLIFE: Sundown Hill – Arltunga (Central Australia) – Through the Gold Light Crystal to Brazil – along the Amazon to Machu Picchu.

TIWI TOTEMS: Sundown Hill – South Sea Islands – Hawaii – Mount Shasta (USA) – Lake Moraine (Canada) – via Eastern Seaboard of USA to Machu Picchu.

HORSE: Sundown Hill – Philippines – China – Mongolia – Tibet – Europe – France – Machu Picchu.

FACING THE NIGHT AND DAY: Sundown Hill – Queensland (Australia) – New Guinea – Japan – North Russia to Finland – Sweden – Norway – Iceland – Tip of Greenland – Machu Picchu.

HABITAT: Sundown Hill via Inner Earth to Machu Picchu.

THOMASINA (JILARRUWI – THE IBIS): Tension Lynch pin between Sundown Hill and Machu Picchu.

HOW TO MAKE YOUR OWN BLESSINGS CHIMES

Blessings Chimes have a triangular wooden top. Inserted into the underside of the wooden triangle are a series of Screw Eyes with a series of chimes dangling from them with THREE 'Strikers' of your own design. The chimes are of different sizes, thicknesses or metals to provide a variety of Tones (which we created by taking apart a number of different, inexpensive, wind chimes). The Screw Eyes are set out in 5 rows from which the Chimes are hung, a single chime at the tip of the triangle, then 2 chimes, then 3 chimes, then 5 chimes and finally 7 chimes. This makes 18 chimes in all. One Screw Eye from which a 'Striker' hangs is placed between rows 2 and 3, and then two Screw Eyes from which 'Strikers' hang are placed between rows 4 and 5.

The 'Strikers' used in creating our Original Blessings Chime for the Marine Meditation had as decorations a Sea horse, a Unicorn, and a Dragon. The Triangular wooden top has a small knob on it, to hold as you shake the Blessings Chimes to create the vibration and resonance.

Although the original has a triangular Top and 18 chimes, you can vary this to your own intuition. The latest version that has been created for David has an Octagonal top and only 8 chimes and is called 'Peace and Harmony Chimes' rather than 'Blessings Chimes' to reflect it's more subtle Sound. Use your imagination and Intuition.

Blessings of Love and Peace

David J Adams

Printed in the United States
By Bookmasters